CONTENTS

Introduction

Directory

Credits

Best Routes

ARCHITECTURE

The Big Sights (route 1) covers architecture of royalty and government, the City (route 9) has Wren churches and steel-and-glass showpieces, and Greenwich (route 19) offers Georgian elegance.

RECOMMENDED ROUTES FOR...

ART FANS

There's something for everyone, from the National Gallery (route 2) and Tate Modern (route 11) to elite Mayfair galleries (route 4). Find the best of British at the National Portrait Gallery (route 2) and Tate Britain (route 11).

COOL BRITANNIA

Find the cutting edge in Soho's bars and clubs (route 3), the boho markets of Portobello Road (route 16) and the fashionable East End (route 17). For Brit Art, visit Tate Britain (route 11).

FAMILIES WITH KIDS

There is plenty for young ones to see: London Zoo (route 6), dinosaurs at the Natural History Museum (route 13), hands-on fun at the Science Museum (route 13) and old buses at the Transport Museum (route 3).

FOOD AND DRINK

The biggest choice is in the West End, from Chinatown to pre-theatre suppers (route 3). For fresh produce visit Borough Market (route 10) and for ethnic cuisine head to the East End (route 17).

LITERARY LONDON

Head to Holborn (route 8) and Bloomsbury (route 7) to follow in the footsteps of Dr Johnson, Charles Dickens and Virginia Woolf; those with poetic sensibilities should visit Hampstead (route 15), home of Keats.

ROYAL LONDON

Have a royal time seeing Buckingham Palace, Changing the Guard and Clarence House (route 1). Kensington Palace and the Albert and Princess Diana memorials are found in Hyde Park (route 12).

SHOPPERS

Shop exhaustively on Oxford Street (route 4), fashionably in Covent Garden (route 3), exclusively in Mayfair (route 4), smartly in Chelsea (route 14) and alternatively in Notting Hill (route 16).

INTRODUCTION

An introduction to London's geography, customs and culture, plus illuminating background information on cuisine, history and what to do when you're there.

Cycling at Hyde Park Corner

EXPLORE LONDON

Fire, plague, population explosions, aerial bombing, economic recessions, urban blight, terrorism… London has taken everything history could throw at it, and this has made it one of the world's most complex and fascinating cities.

There must be something special about London to attract more than 27 million overnight visitors each year. And it is not the weather. There are, however, wonderful palaces and cathedrals, theatres and museums, parks and gardens, restaurants serving cuisine from all parts of the world, a vibrant nightlife, and a refreshingly cosmopolitan and open attitude towards diversity in all things, especially its own inhabitants.

POPULATION

Population growth

The population of London is estimated at around 8.2 million people and there is no sign of any let up in its growth. London is generally considered the most populous city in the European Union (EU). Of course, there are questions over where the boundaries of London's sprawl lie, but it is usually defined as the financial district ('the City') and the 32 boroughs that constitute 'Greater London'.

The population on this territory rose from about 1.1 million in 1801 to peak at over 8.6 million in 1939. It then declined to 6.7 million in 1988, before growing once more to about the same level today as in 1970 (also the level of the 1920s). However, the wider metropolitan area of London continues to spread outwards and is now home to between 12 and 14 million, depending on the definition of that area.

Ethnicity

More than one in three London residents is from a minority ethnic group. Figures from the Office for National Statistics show that, as of the 2011 census, London's foreign-born population is 3.7 million (45 percent), up from 1.6 million in 1997. Of this number, about 39 percent are from the Indian subcontinent and about 35 percent are African or Afro-Caribbean. In addition, there has recently been an influx of hundreds of thousands of workers from the new member countries of the EU, particularly Poland.

Of course, London has been a focus of immigration for centuries, whether as a place of safety (as with the Huguenots fleeing Catholic France, or Eastern European Jews escaping Nazism) or for economic reasons (as with the Irish, Bangladeshis and West Indians).

Grosvenor Square Garden   *Crossing the Millennium Bridge*

Wealth distribution

London ranks as one of the most expensive cities in the world, alongside Tokyo and Moscow. At one end of the scale, London is ranked third in the world in number of billionaire residents. There is also the City of London, renowned for awarding stellar bonuses to its star employees.

At the other end of the scale are the down-and-outs sleeping rough in shop doorways, and newly arrived economic immigrants living in cramped boarding houses. In the past, the East End hosted countless impoverished arrivals from overseas. Many have subsequently moved elsewhere in

Soldier near Westminster Abbey

London as they have gained prosperity. A higher percentage of Indians and Pakistanis, for example, now own their own homes in the capital than white people.

THE CLIMATE

London has a mild climate. Snow (other than a light dusting) and temperatures below freezing are fairly unusual, with January temperatures averaging 4°C (39°F). In the summer months, temperatures average 17°C (63°F), but can rise much higher, causing the city to become stiflingly hot (air conditioning is not universal). Heat stored by the city's buildings creates a microclimate with temperatures up to 5 °C (9 °F) warmer in the city than in the surrounding areas. Even so, summer temperatures rarely rise much above 33 °C (91.4 °F), and the highest temperature ever recorded in London was 38.1 °C (100.6 °F), measured at Kew Gardens during the European heat wave of 2003.

Day to day fluctuations can be significant, though, and surprise showers catch people unprepared all year round. This enables people to engage in a favourite topic of conversation and to tut-tut over inclement spells. Whatever the season, visitors should come prepared with wet-weather clothes (a mackintosh or other waterproof coat) and other useful apparatus (umbrella, hat, etc).

Girls in Camden

LONDON GEOGRAPHY

The political map

When people talk about London, they are usually referring to the area covered by Greater London. This administrative organisation was imposed on the city in 1965. It comprises the City of London and 32 London boroughs.

Originally, there were two cities here: the City of Westminster (centred on the Houses of Parliament and Westminster Abbey) and the City of London (often referred to as simply 'the City', and covering what is now the financial district – the historic square mile between St Paul's Cathedral and the Tower of London). Westminster is now a borough just like any other, governed by a borough council. The City of London, on the other hand, has its own unique institutions of local government dating back to the 12th century: the Corporation of London, headed by the Lord Mayor.

Presiding over Greater London at the top level is the Greater London Authority (GLA) with, at its head, a directly elected mayor (not to be confused with the Lord Mayor of the City of London). The Mayor and the GLA are responsible for the Metropolitan Police Authority, the London Fire and Emergency Planning Authority,

DON'T LEAVE LONDON WITHOUT...

Indulging in an afternoon tea. London has no shortage of posh hotels and charming restaurants where you can enjoy a traditional British afternoon tea. The Wolseley is a good bet. See page 45.

Strolling through one of the parks. London is crowded and noisy, but luckily it's easy to find a green escape. St James's, Green and Regent's are all delightful, but our pick is the lovely expanse of Hyde Park. See page 72.

Admiring royal pageantry. The best way to immerse yourself in royal London is to watch the iconic Changing the Guard ceremony at Buckingham Palace. See page 32.

Cruising down the Thames. A river trip is a great way to get your bearings in London. Combine it with some culture and catch the boat between the two world-class Tate galleries. See page 68.

Browsing the Sunday markets. The East End is the place to be on Sunday mornings, when you can pick up bargains and mingle with hipsters at Spitalfields for fashions and jewellery and Columbia Road for plants and flowers. See page 88.

Enjoying a great view of the city. There's nothing quite like taking in London from above. Scale the Monument, the OXO Tower or the Shard – or best of all, take a trip on the London Eye. See page 63.

Drinking in a historic pub. Nursing a pint in a traditional boozer is a must. The best option is the timewarped Ye Olde Cheshire Cheese, off Fleet Street. See page 55.

Relaxing on the South Bank　　　　　　　　　　*Portobello Market stall*

the London Development Agency and Transport for London. Services such as refuse disposal, housing grants and parking control are run at local level by the boroughs.

North–South, East–West

Whatever the political subdivisions of London, the physical and social ones are often more significant. Not least of these is the River Thames, dividing the city into north and south. London north of the river has historically been the location of government and commerce. The south, apart from the river banks themselves, was less developed until the 19th century, when it became a vast residential suburb.

The London Eye

South London is still much less of a destination for a day out than north London, and cab drivers, notoriously, sometimes refuse to take passengers south of the river.

West London, especially Mayfair, Kensington and Chelsea, is the posh end of town. It is now particularly popular with wealthy foreign residents, attracted by the relative security of the area, the investment potential of owning one of its smart properties, and Britain's lenient tax regime. East London, on the other hand, has historically harboured some of the poorest communities in the city, with the indigenous working classes, close by London's docks, living alongside newly arrived immigrants. Parts of it are now far more vibrant than west London, popular with artists and a younger, more outward-looking generation.

HEAVEN AND HELL

The 18th-century man of letters, Samuel Johnson, famously declared, 'When a man is tired of London, he is tired of life; for there is in London all that life can afford.' This is still the case today: London offers some the chance to accumulate great wealth, others to be at the centre of cultural ferment, and many others the opportunity simply to be themselves in a tolerant and civilised environment (no matter what their creed or colour, sexual orientation or chosen lifestyle).

Playing boules in Clerkenwell

However, at times, London has seemed less than idyllic. In 1819, the poet Shelley wrote, 'Hell is a city much like London/A populous and smoky city.' Indeed, at one time, the streets in the old City were so dark and narrow that shopkeepers had to erect mirrors outside their windows to reflect light into the shops. And pollution and congestion are still problems today, warranting the city's widely used nickname, 'The Big Smoke'.

The last 25 years, though, have seen something of a renaissance for the city, with the regeneration of neglected areas, a vibrant art and music scene, fuller employment, and even some improvements in public transport. This atmosphere of optimism and confidence reached its apogee in the late '90s, when London was the centre of what the media referred to as 'Cool Britannia', and was a magnet for many an aspiring mover and shaker; and then again in 2012 when it played host to the Olympic Games.

London cabbies

About 25,000 drivers work in London, half of them as owner-drivers. The others either hire vehicles from big fleets or work night shifts in someone else's cab. Would-be drivers must register with the Public Carriage Office and then spend up to four years learning London in minute detail – known as 'the Knowledge'. They achieve this by travelling the streets of the metropolis on a moped, whatever the weather, working out a multitude of routes from a clipboard mounted on the handlebars. So even if the supposedly garrulous cabbies do not always know what they are talking about, they do know where they are going. The classic cab itself – or Hackney Carriage, as it is officially known – is the FX4, launched in 1959, and still going strong in its updated incarnation (with full wheelchair access). The traditional manner for hailing a cab is to raise your arm and shout, 'Taxi!' The cab may not always stop though: Prince Philip and the comedian Stephen Fry are known to maintain their own black cabs, so that they can travel around the city in anonymity.

A London cabbie

Central Saint Martins, King's Cross

TOP TIPS FOR EXPLORING LONDON

Camden. North of Euston Station is Camden, where many famous bands played their first gigs. Try Barfly, the Jazz Café, the Dublin Castle, or the Bull and Gate. There is also a huge alternative clothes market around Camden Lock.

Dance. For ballet, London's major venues are the Royal Opera House and the London Coliseum, home to the Royal Ballet and English National Ballet respectively. For contemporary dance, the main venue is Sadler's Wells, in Islington, to the north of the City.

The Royal Mews. Visit the Royal Mews on Buckingham Palace Road to see the Queen's horses, carriages and motor cars used for coronations, state visits, weddings and other events.

Bloomsbury Group. In the early 20th century, a group of friends including E.M. Forster, Lytton Strachey, J.M. Keynes, Clive and Vanessa Bell, Duncan Grant and Virginia and Leonard Woolf would meet at each other's houses at Nos 37, 46, 50 and 51 Gordon Square to discuss literature and art. Other notable Bloomsbury residents have included Thomas Carlyle at 38 Ampton Street, Edgar Allan Poe at 83 Southampton Row, Anthony Trollope at 6 Store Street and W.B. Yeats at 5 Upper Woburn Place.

Wellcome Collection. Opposite Euston Station is the excellent Wellcome Collection (www.wellcome collection.org), a museum/ art space devoted to medicine and its relationships with art and society.

Tower Bridge. Next to the Tower of London is Tower Bridge (www.towerbridge.org. uk). The high-level walkways offer wonderful views to the paying public.

Imperial War Museum. This museum that chronicles the horrors of modern war (Lambeth Road; www.iwm.org.uk) is housed in a former hospital for the insane.

Globe Productions. The season of this South Bank open-air theatre runs from May to early October. If you have a bargain standing ticket, bring waterproofs in case of downpours; umbrellas are not allowed.

18 Folgate Street. Two streets beyond Spitalfields Market is Dennis Severs' House (www.dennissevershouse.co.uk). In 1967, Severs moved from his native California and bought this silk weaver's house and recreated its 18th-century state. It is now as if the original family have just left the room, leaving a half-eaten scone and a smouldering fire.

ArcelorMittal Orbit. In the Olympic Park (tube: Stratford) is Anish Kapoor's sculptural tribute to the Olympics. From April 2014 visitors can ascend to the viewing platform and enjoy spectacular views over the park and the city beyond.

Hampton Court. In summer, you could visit Kew Gardens in the morning and Hampton Court in the afternoon. Boats leave Kew at noon and 1pm for Hampton Court and return at 3pm and 4pm, subject to tides. For more information see www. wpsa.co.uk.

Eating at a Shoreditch café

FOOD AND DRINK

London's cuisine was once reputed to offer little more than overcooked stodge. Not so now: as well as impressive renditions of just about every other country's cuisine, you can appreciate the finest of Britain's own food heritage.

The last few decades have seen a remarkable transformation in London's restaurant scene, bringing it into the international league. Londoners' taste for innovative cooking of the best produce has made the city the envy of foreign capitals more traditionally regarded as gastronomically blessed. At one time, however, things were very different, and British food was the butt of many jokes, especially from the French. Jacques Chirac is quoted as saying that 'you can't trust people who cook as badly as that'. Nowadays, a good pork chop from St John or Scottish lobster at Gordon Ramsay would have him eating his words.

BRITISH CUISINE

As well as a great enthusiasm for foreign styles of cooking, the blossoming of London's restaurant scene is closely related to the re-evaluation of Britain's indigenous cuisine. A new generation of energetic head chefs has proved emphatically that British food is much more than meat and two veg, a stodgy pie full of gravy or a buttie stuffed with soggy chips. Now you can find Cromer crab, Cornish sprats, Gressingham duck,

juicy Herdwick lamb, Galloway beef, and traditional desserts such as Eccles cakes with Lancashire cheese or bread-and-butter pudding. This new-found culinary zeal has filtered down to the local pub, where potted shrimps, shepherd's pie, Lancashire hotpot and bangers and mash are cooked with care and served with pride.

PLACES TO EAT

High-end restaurants

As well as long-established stalwarts such as Le Gavroche, in recent years London has nurtured numerous other Michelin-star contenders. Gordon Ramsay, Marcus Wareing, Tom Aikens, and Angela Hartnett among others have all raised expectations of what restaurants should be offering.

The food at many top restaurants is based on French cooking techniques. Even the so-called 'modern British' style is founded on a combination of high-quality British ingredients with French methods of preparation. For interesting alternatives try the River Café, with its unpretentious modern Italian cooking, or Benares for innovative Indian dishes.

Japanese food is popular

Retro food van, South Bank

It is easily argued that many restaurants in London give too much emphasis to design and image and not enough to the food itself. At Sketch or China Tang for example, some feel that if the food is fairly good, it is so as not to distract from the interior decoration. A step further are the likes of The Ivy, where it is the other diners, some of them celebrities, that are the focus of attention.

Many of the restaurants mentioned above require booking weeks, perhaps months, in advance. Beware also, if they take your credit card details when you book, you may be charged anyway if you do not then show up.

Pubs

If all this business of booking weeks ahead, hefty bills and embarrassing formality is more than you can take, do not fret; all is not lost. Many of the best eating experiences in London are quite inexpensive, relaxed affairs.

A major component of British social history is the public house, which in recent years has been re-evaluated. There is a lot to be said for a pie and a pint. For pub food is a distinctive cuisine in itself (and that does not mean ploughman's lunch with a limp lettuce leaf and a wedge of cheese). Think of steak-and-kidney pudding, meat loaf, Lancashire hotpot, shepherd's pie, sausage and mash and the traditional Sunday roast. If well executed, these dishes can be delicious.

Lots of traditional pubs have now been converted into 'gastro-pubs', many of them sensitively, some crassly. The cliché is of a pub desecrated: its centuries-old patina stripped away, floorboards sanded down, walls painted white, shabby-chic furniture brought in and a blackboard advertising faux-Mediterranean dishes.

However, when it is done well, the gastro-pub can be very good. Try The Anchor and Hope in Southwark, or The Coach and Horses on the edge of the City, or The Cow on Westbourne Park Road near Notting Hill.

Ethnic restaurants

Another mainstay of London's culinary heritage is the huge variety of ethnic restaurants, especially Indian, Chinese, Japanese, Vietnamese and Thai. According to city authorities, 53 major country styles are represented among the 6,000 licensed restaurants. Visit Kingsland Road in the East End for Vietnamese and Turkish, Whitechapel or Tooting (south London) for Indian, and Stockwell (also south of the river) for Portuguese establishments.

Greasy spoons, pie and mash, and fish and chips

Often overlooked is London's fast-disappearing old-fashioned, working-class grub. Even 15 years ago there was always a haven close at hand offering a plate of piping hot food at everyday prices. Now, the greasy spoon caffs, fish

Borough Market

and chip, and pie and mash shops are being usurped by coffee bars and fast-food corporations that can pay grasping landlords' higher rents.

'Greasy spoon' cafés serve all-day breakfasts: eggs, bacon, chips and beans, sometimes with manly extras such as black pudding or bubble and squeak. Also, strong tea and white bread and butter. Check out www.classiccafes.co.uk for an anthology of the best greasy spoon caffs still open.

Pie and mash shops serve meat pies or eels (jellied or stewed) with liquor (an odd sort of glop based on parsley sauce) and mashed potato. The premises themselves have wonderful tiled interiors, marble-topped tables and wooden benches. Good examples are Manze's on Tower Bridge Road and F. Cooke on Broadway Market in the East End.

Lastly come the fish and chip shops, with their fat stubby fried potatoes, quite impossible to replicate in a conventional kitchen, and fish in batter, double fried. Try Fryer's Delight on Theobald's Road (see Restaurants) and

Rock & Sole Plaice in Covent Garden (see route 3).

Chains

London has ever more chain restaurants, more indeed than most other European cities. Some are good (Wahaca or Leon for example), others are bland and disappointing.

DRINKS

Beer

Traditionally, beer was to Britain what wine was to France. It comes in various forms, from lager (now the most popular form in Britain) to ale (brewed using only top-fermenting yeasts; sweeter and fuller bodied) to stout (creamy, almost coffee-like beer made from roasted malts or roast barley), of which the most famous brand is probably Guinness.

Pubs generally serve beer either 'draught' or from the cask. In the case of the former, a keg is pressurised with carbon-dioxide gas, which drives the beer to the dispensing tap. For the latter, beer is pulled from the cask via a beer line with a hand pump at the bar. This method is generally used for what is often termed 'real ale': unfiltered and unpasteurised beer, which, unlike industrially produced lagers, requires careful storage at the correct temperature.

Wine

The popularity of wine-drinking in Britain has increased dramatically in the

---

Food and Drink Prices

Price guide for an average two-course meal for one with a glass of house wine throughout this book:

££££ = over £40
£££ = £25–£40
££ = £15–25
£ = below £15

A tasty paella   *A Leadenhall Market pub*

last few decades. In the unenlightened days, many pubs served only Liebfraumilch or Lambrusco, but nowadays you can expect a more grown-up selection, and New World wines are at least as widely offered by pubs as European wines. The growing popularity of wine in Britain has even encouraged some growers to start producing English varieties. Try the restaurant Roast, upstairs at Borough Market (see route 10), for a good-quality selection of English wines.

Cider
A longer-established English tipple is cider, produced in southwest England since before the Romans arrived. Made from the fermented juice of apples, it is also known as 'scrumpy' (windfalls are 'scrumps'). The pear equivalent is called 'perry'. Unfortunately, many pubs only offer mass-produced cider made from apple concentrate. For the real thing, try The Blackfriar (see route 8), The Harp on Chandos Place, tucked just behind St-Martin-in-the-Fields (see route 1), or Chimes restaurant on Churton Street in Pimlico.

Whisky
Another speciality is whisky, produced in Scotland and Ireland. This is available as 'single malt' (malt whisky from a single distillery), as well as 'blended' – cheaper whiskies are normally made from a mixture of malt and grain whiskies from many distilleries. Most pubs

in central London will offer a small selection of both, though aficionados may consider joining the Whisky Society, which has its members' rooms above the Bleeding Heart Restaurant in Hatton Garden, Clerkenwell (Bleeding Heart Yard; www.smws.co.uk).

Last orders
Most pubs ring a bell for 'last orders' at 11pm and then expect you to drink up and depart by 11.30pm. In 2003 new legislation was introduced allowing pub landlords to apply for extended opening hours, up to 24 hours a day, seven days a week. In practice (although many now stay open throughout the afternoon), only a small minority of pubs made such an application. However, this has not stopped renewed concern about Britain's supposed 'binge-drinking' culture.

Food markets

Perhaps the best of London's food markets for the visitor is Borough Market near London Bridge (Thur 11am–5pm, Fri noon–6pm, Sat 8am–5pm). It offers some of the country's best produce in an historic setting. For other farmers' markets, see www.lfm.org.uk. London's main wholesale markets are Smithfields for meat (Mon–Fri from 3am; guided tours once a month), Billingsgate for fish (now in Docklands; Tue–Sat 4–9.30am) and Spitalfields for fruit and vegetables (now in Leyton; Mon–Sat midnight–11am).

Lobb's the bootmakers

SHOPPING

Napoleon called England a nation of shopkeepers. Perhaps he had a point. Whether you are in the market for a grand piano or a custom-made brassiere, a pet parrot or a snuff box, there will be somewhere in London you can buy it.

With more than 30,000 shops, and everything available, from Old Masters to vintage film posters, Savile Row suits to punk-rock T-shirts, London is an easy place to spend your cash. And just to make it even easier, unlike in many other European capitals, Sundays and summer holidays are not sacred: this is a year-round shopper's destination.

SHOPPING AREAS

For those on a retail mission, the sheer size of the city means you have to be selective. However, London's shopping geography is relatively easy to navigate and can be loosely divided into shopping districts, each offering a distinctive experience. Indeed, in some cases there are whole streets devoted to one theme: Savile Row and Jermyn Street for gentlemen's outfitters, Hatton Garden for jewellery, Carnaby Street for branded street fashion.

The best means for getting from area to area is usually the tube, though for the journey home, those laden with heavy bags may favour a taxi. The bus network has good coverage, but is slower and less easy to navigate. And of course, there is always a lot to be said for walking: distances between some streets – Oxford Street and Piccadilly, Regent Street and Bond Street – are short enough to walk.

Designer districts

For those wanting the best of European and international designer fashions, Knightsbridge, home to the higher-end department stores Harrods and Harvey Nichols, has perhaps the highest concentration of such shops. Haute couture names from Armani to Yves Saint Laurent sit next to established British designers Katharine Hamnett, Anya Hindmarch and Bruce Oldfield, to name a few. Also out west are the King's Road and Fulham Road in Chelsea, with couturiers such as Anne Fontaine and Amanda Wakeley sandwiched between smart interior design stores.

Bond Street, in Mayfair, also offers a vast choice of designer labels as well as the world's biggest names in jewellery, and some of London's top dealers in Old Masters and antique furniture. Cork Street, the next road along, is lined with

The Harrods food hall   *Directional vests, Camden Market*

dealers in modern art, while a little further east still is Savile Row.

Around Piccadilly

Around the Piccadilly area are some of London's oldest shops, many of which hold royal warrants to supply the Queen and her family with goods. On Piccadilly itself are up-market grocer Fortnum & Mason and Hatchards the booksellers. Parallel with Piccadilly is Jermyn Street, which specialises in shirts, though it is also the place for the debonair to find a silk dressing gown or a pair of monogrammed carpet slippers. On St James's, just nearby, is Lock's the hatters, and Lobb's the bootmakers. Then there is Regent Street, the world's first purpose-built shopping street, running north from Piccadilly Circus, and home to Britain's largest toy shop, Hamleys, as well as Liberty, the Arts and Crafts shopping institution.

Chains and department stores

High-street chains and department stores characterise Oxford Street, the capital's main shopping thoroughfare. Selfridges and John Lewis, near Bond Street tube, are perhaps the only destination shops here. Near Oxford Circus, running south, is Carnaby Street. Finally, at the eastern end of Oxford Street is Tottenham Court Road, dominated by electronics and hi-fi shops, as well as home furnishings stores, including Habitat and Heal's.

Soho and Covent Garden

Although Soho has never quite lost its seedy atmosphere, in between the sex shops there are some fine delicatessens, as well as stores selling hip urban wear. Bookworms should head for nearby Charing Cross Road (and Cecil Court, too), with its second-hand bookshops and major branches of large book chains.

Covent Garden offers high-street and urban fashion as well as specialist emporia dedicated to teapots or kites or cheese or wooden toys.

Markets

London has markets for antiques, crafts, clothes and, of course, food (see Food and Drink). For antiques enthusiasts, Portobello Road is the obvious choice, with the main market held on Saturdays. An alternative is Alfies Antique Market (Tue–Sat 10am–6pm) on Church Street near Marylebone. For a more up-market affair, try the shops on Kensington Church Street, where more than 80 dealers display their finds.

For clothes and crafts, in the East End there are weekend markets at Spitalfields and Brick Lane, as well as the weekday rag trade in Petticoat Lane (also Sunday morning). Then there is Portobello Road (retro) and Camden Lock (retro, clubwear, goth and punk). At Greenwich market (Tue–Sun; stalls vary on different days) the emphasis is on crafts and deli foods.

Henry VIII at Shakespeare's Globe

ENTERTAINMENT

Whether you prefer to get engrossed in the latest cinematic release, listen to a world-class rendition of Mahler, enjoy classic drama, a lively musical, or the latest R&B, London can offer the appropriate venue.

An international city such as London is large and densely populated enough to support a bewildering variety of entertainment venues.

THEATRE

London's Theatreland is in the West End – in particular around Piccadilly, Shaftesbury Avenue, Charing Cross Road, The Strand and Covent Garden. Here, the tradition is as much about the theatres themselves as the quality of the drama. This is where velvet-and-gilt Victorian playhouses were designed so that most of the audience would peer down over the stage, where 'the gods' (the seats high at the back) bring on vertigo, and where it is difficult to escape the concern that, had the buildings been conceived today, fire regulations would have ensured that they never left the architects' drawing boards.

Nevertheless, the West End is still a theatrical magnet, because this is where the money is. Catering for audiences by the coach-load, impresarios look to musical spectacles, revivals, and to plays that will please the widest range of tastes. As a result, such middle-of-the-road creative

types as composer Andrew Lloyd Webber and producer Cameron Mackintosh have become both famous and very rich.

Drama old and new

Many theatre lovers claim that the mania for musicals squeezes out new drama productions. Yet a glance through the theatre listings doesn't entirely bear out this claim. Classics are interpreted anew at the Donmar Warehouse in Covent Garden and at the National Theatre and Old and Young Vic just south of the river; and Shakespeare's Globe has been a triumph of culture over commercialism. Meanwhile, new writing is still put on at the Royal Court, and experimental work and alternative comedy are mounted at numerous fringe theatres.

MUSIC

London has an active and varied music scene, with plenty to cater to every musical taste. For the latest music, the clubs and bars of Camden in North London are good hunting grounds for up-and-coming bands. Many famous artists played their first gigs at Barfly, for example, and young hopefuls continue

Last Night of the Proms

to do so today. If, on the other hand, jazz is more your style, then Ronnie Scott's in Soho is the best-known venue, showcasing top international artists.

Classical music enthusiasts will find numerous professional orchestras in the capital. Perhaps the best at the moment is the London Symphony Orchestra, which usually performs at the Barbican. Several of the other orchestras – including the Philharmonia – are based at the Royal Festival Hall on the South Bank. Then in the summer, there is the BBC-sponsored Proms festival of around 100 concerts at the Royal Albert Hall in South Kensington. Many of the world's greatest orchestras and soloists feature in the line ups, while the famous Last Night is performed by the redoubtable BBC Symphony Orchestra.

For opera enthusiasts, there are the Royal Opera and English National Opera companies. The Royal Opera House in Covent Garden, home to the Royal Opera, is a magnificent theatre presenting lavish performances in the original language. Tickets are expensive, unless you are prepared to stand or accept a distant view. English National Opera's home is the London Coliseum on St Martin's Lane. Ticket prices are lower than at Covent Garden and can sometimes be bought on the night of a performance.

FILM

If you want to see the latest Hollywood blockbusters in Central London, the place to go is Leicester Square (see route 3), where the big multiplex cinemas are clustered. Ticket prices are high, but audiences benefit from the high-quality projection and sound systems. If arthouse cinema is more your style, just a short walk north, in Soho, is the main branch of the Curzon cinema chain (www.curzoncinemas.com), which shows all the latest releases.

Meanwhile, south of the river at the Southbank Centre is the British Film Institute, a government-subsidised organisation that screens classic and cult films of the past, and organises film festivals and themed seasons. The BFI also runs the Imax cinema near Waterloo Station, which shows blockbuster, animated, and 3-D films on its vast screen.

NIGHTLIFE

London has several nightlife scenes. Hoxton and Shoreditch in the East End are home to the hippest nightspots, where DJ bars and 'pop-up' nightclubs are congregated. For large-scale clubs featuring the latest popular music, Leicester Square and Covent Garden are the main destinations. Camden (see left) is a good option for live-music venues. The gay clubbing scene is concentrated in Vauxhall, south of the river, while Soho's Old Compton and Brewer streets accommodate many gay pubs and cabaret venues.

HISTORY: KEY DATES

From humble beginnings, through sacking, fire, pestilence and war, and with renowned pomp and circumstance, London has grown to become one of the world's most culturally vibrant, cosmopolitan and ethnically diverse capitals.

EARLY PERIOD

AD 43	Emperor Claudius establishes the trade port of Londinium and builds a bridge over the River Thames.
61	Boudicca sacks the city but is defeated, and London is rebuilt.
***c.*200**	City wall built. London is made the capital of Britannia Superior.
410	Romans withdraw to defend Rome. London falls into decline.
604	The first St Paul's Cathedral is founded by King Ethelbert.
***c.*750**	The monastery of St Peter is founded on Thorney Island; it later becomes Westminster Abbey.
884	London becomes the capital under Alfred the Great.
1042	Edward the Confessor moves his court to Westminster.

AFTER THE CONQUEST

1066	William I, Duke of Normandy, conquers Britain.
1078	Tower of London's White Tower is built.
1348–9	Black Death wipes out about 50 percent of London's population.
1534	Henry VIII declares himself head of the Church of England.
1558–1603	London is the capital of a mighty kingdom under Elizabeth I.
1599	The Globe theatre opens at Bankside.
1605	Guy Fawkes attempts to blow up James I and Parliament.
1664–6	Plague hits London again, killing around 110,000 citizens.
1666	Great Fire of London destroys 80 percent of London's buildings.

AFTER THE FIRE

1675	Sir Christopher Wren begins to rebuild St Paul's Cathedral.
1783	Last execution held at Tyburn (Marble Arch).

Historic view of London

| 1834 | Building starts on the Houses of Parliament that are still standing today, after the old Palace of Westminster burns down. |

THE AGE OF EMPIRE

1837–1901	Queen Victoria's reign, characterised by Empire building and the Industrial Revolution.
1849	Henry Charles Harrod opens a shop in Knightsbridge.
1851	The hugely successful Great Exhibition is held in architect Joseph Paxton's Crystal Palace in Hyde Park.
1859	'Big Ben' bell is hung in the tower of the Palace of Westminster.
1863	London Underground opens its first line, the Metropolitan line.
1888	The serial murderer dubbed Jack the Ripper strikes in Whitechapel.

20TH CENTURY

1914–18	World War I. Zeppelins bomb London.
1939–45	World War II. London is heavily bombed.
1951	Festival of Britain. Southbank Centre built adjacent to Waterloo.
1960s	London christened the capital of hip for fashion, music and the arts.
1980s	Margaret Thatcher years. Several IRA bombs hit London.
1986	The Greater London Council is abolished by Thatcher.
1997	New Labour elected under Tony Blair. 'Cool Britannia' period.

21ST CENTURY

2000	Dome, London Eye, Tate Modern and Jubilee Line extension open to celebrate the millennium. Ken Livingstone elected mayor.
2001	Greater London Authority is re-established under Mayor Livingstone.
2005	Terrorist bomb attacks on 7 July kill 52 and injure about 700.
2008	Boris Johnson elected mayor.
2012	London celebrates the Queen's Diamond Jubilee and hosts the Olympic Games.
2013	London Underground marks the 150th anniversary of the first tube journey.

BEST ROUTES

Lion on Trafalgar Square

THE BIG SIGHTS

In a changing world it's reassuring that Nelson is still on his column in Trafalgar Square, the prime minister's at No. 10 Downing Street, Big Ben is chiming at the Houses of Parliament and the Queen is at Buckingham Palace.

> **DISTANCE:** 3 miles (5km)
> **TIME:** A full day
> **START:** Trafalgar Square
> **END:** Buckingham Palace

This is the route to do if you are new to London or if you want to revisit the capital's major royal and political sights.

TRAFALGAR SQUARE

Trafalgar Square ❶ is plumb in the centre of London, as attested to by the plaque on the traffic island in the south of the square. It was conceived by the Prince Regent in 1820, was designed in its current form by Sir Charles Barry in 1838, and assumed its current name in 1841 in commemoration of Nelson's victory over Napoleon's navy at the Battle of Trafalgar in 1805.

Nelson's Column

At the centre of the square is **Nelson's Column**, a 151ft (46m) granite pillar topped by an 18ft (5.5m) statue of Admi-

ral Lord Nelson. Battle-scarred, with only one arm (though without a patch on his blind eye), he gazes south, surveying the fleet of miniature ships atop the flag poles lining the Mall. Completed in 1843, the column was designed by William Railton, the statue by E.H. Baily. The four iconic lions at the base were added in 1867 by Edwin Landseer, cast from the metal of the cannons of the defeated French fleet.

Flanking the column are two fountains: the originals were replaced in 1939 with larger ones, by Edwin Lutyens, allegedly to limit the space for political demonstrations. In the corners of the square are plinths, with statues of General Charles Napier, Major General Sir Henry Havelock and George IV (astride a horse without a saddle, boots or stirrups); the fourth plinth, originally left empty, is used to display contemporary artworks.

Bordering the square

Around the square, Canada House, South Africa House and Uganda House are memories of distant Empire

St Martin-in-the-Fields *Trafalgar Square at night*

days. On the north side of the square is the **National Gallery** ❷ (covered in detail in route 2), which displays pre-20th-century art. On the lawn in front is a statue of James II by Grinling Gibbons. Hand on hip, he is inexplicably dressed as an ancient Roman. Further along is a diminutive statue of George Washington, a gift from the state of Virginia. He stands on soil imported from the US, honouring his declaration that he would never again set foot on British soil.

St Martin-in-the-Fields

On the east side of the square is **St Martin-in-the-Fields** ❸ (www.stmartin-in-the-fields.org; Mon–Sat 8.30am–6pm (closed 1–2pm Mon–Fri), Sun 3.30–5.30pm; free). A church has stood here since the 13th century, when this area was fields between the City of Westminster and the City of London.

The present church was completed in 1726 to designs by James Gibbs. His amalgam of classical and Baroque styles subsequently became

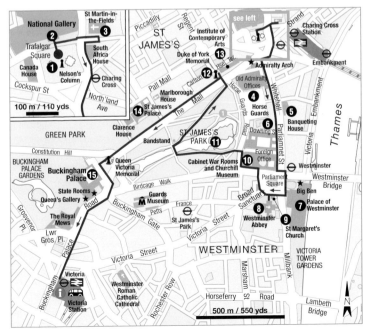

Houses of Parliament

the model for many churches in the US. The church was largely paid for by George III, and it remains Buckingham Palace's parish church; the box to the left of the gallery is reserved for the royal family.

The church is a venue for concerts of classical music. It also has a Brass Rubbing Centre and a good café. The churchyard outside is the burial site of Charles II's mistress Nell Gwynn, William Hogarth and Joshua Reynolds.

WHITEHALL

Leave Trafalgar Square and head south down Whitehall, named after Henry VIII's palace, which burnt down in 1698. Most of the monumental buildings on this street are government departments, beginning with former Admiralty buildings on your right and the Ministry of Defence on your left.

Horse Guards

On the right, through an arch, is **Horse Guards ❹**, where the Household Cavalry, the Queen's bodyguard on state occasions, mounts the daily Changing the Guard ceremony (www.changing-the-guard.com; Mon–Sat 11am, Sun 10am; free). Cameras click, horses nod, commands are shouted, then the troop returns to barracks.

Banqueting House

On the opposite side of Whitehall from Horse Guards is the **Banquet-**ing House ❺ (www. hrp.org.uk; Mon–Sat 10am–5pm; charge). It was built by Inigo Jones for James I as part of Whitehall Palace in 1619–22 and was probably London's first building made of Portland stone, and first in the classically influenced style of the 16th-century Italian architect Andrea Palladio. It must have looked astonishingly avant-garde among the Tudor timber-and-brick buildings surrounding it (these burnt down in 1698).

Inside, the Rubens ceiling provides a robust contrast to the restraint of the exterior. Commissioned by Charles I to glorify his father James I, it celebrates the divine right of the Stuart kings. However, a bust over the entrance commemorates the fact that Charles was beheaded just outside in 1649.

Downing Street

On the opposite side of the road, and further along, is **Downing Street ❻**, home to the prime minister of the day since 1732. Traditionally, the prime minister lives at No. 10, and the chancellor at No. 11. Since 1989, steel gates have closed the street to the public for security reasons.

PARLIAMENT SQUARE

Now continue down Whitehall, passing, on your right, the **Foreign Office**, designed by George Gilbert Scott in Italianate style and completed in 1868, before coming to Parliament Square.

Changing the Guard

Horse Guards

On your left is the **Palace of West-minster** ❼, where the two Houses of Parliament (the House of Lords and the House of Commons) meet. Visitors can attend debates, watch judicial hearings and committees, and take guided tours of the building (tel: 0844-847 1672; www.parliament.uk; charge).

Tickets may sometimes be available on the day from the office next to the Jewel Tower in Old Palace Yard, opposite.

Monarchs from Edward the Confessor (1003–66) to Henry VIII (1491–1547) have had residences at this location, which is still a royal palace. The oldest part surviving today is Westminster Hall, the walls of which date from 1097; once used as a law court, it was the scene of the trial of the Gunpowder Plot conspirators in 1606. Henry VIII also apparently used it for playing tennis.

The rest of the old palace was almost completely burnt down in a fire in 1834 – the crypt of St Stephen's Chapel and the Jewel Tower survived. Rebuilding took just over 30 years, according to the neo-Gothic plans of Sir Charles Barry and A.W. Pugin.

During World War II, however, a bombing raid destroyed the chamber of the House of Commons, so architect Sir Giles Gilbert Scott was commissioned to design the replacement. Today the vast building contains nearly 1,200 rooms, 100 staircases and more than 2 miles (3km) of corridors.

Westminster Abbey

Across the road from the Houses of Parliament, on the south side of the square, is **Westminster Abbey** ❽ (www.westminster-abbey.org; main abbey church: Mon, Tue, Thu, Fri, Sat 9.30am–3.30pm, Wed 9.30am–6pm; Chapter House and museum: daily 10.30am–4pm; cloisters: daily 8am–6pm; charge). The medieval abbey on this site was completed and consecrated in 1065, only a week before Edward the Confessor's death. He, along with almost all monarchs since, was buried here. King Harold and William the Conqueror were subsequently crowned here on St Edward's Chair – again, as have most monarchs since.

Henry III rebuilt the abbey in the 13th century, and only the Pyx chamber (royal treasury) and undercroft remain of the original. The fan-vaulted Henry VII Chapel was added from 1503 to 1512, and architect Nicholas Hawksmoor built the west towers in 1745.

Among the church's many relics and monuments is St Edward the Confessor's burial vault, rediscovered in 2005 beneath the mosaic pavement, before the High Altar. Also of note is the Chapter House, with its fine 13th-century tiled pavement, and, further on, the Little Cloister and College Garden.

St Margaret's

Next door is the official church of the House of Commons, **St Margaret's** ❾ (Mon–Fri 9.30am–3.30pm, Sat 9.30am–1.30pm, Sun 2–4.30pm; free).

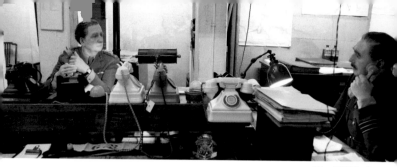

Churchill War Rooms

Inside, the fine east window (1526) commemorates the marriage of Henry VIII and Catherine of Aragon, while the west window (1888) is a tribute to Sir Walter Raleigh (1552–1618), executed for treason nearby. He is buried in the chancel.

Churchill War Rooms

Leaving Parliament Square by Great George Street, you come to the edge of St James's Park. Turn right, and on the corner of King Charles Street are the **Churchill War Rooms** ⑩ (www.iwm. org.uk; daily 9.30am–6pm; charge), the underground bunker from which Winston Churchill masterminded his World War II campaign.

Little has changed since it was closed on 16 August 1945; every book, map, chart and pin remains in place, as does the BBC microphone Churchill used for his famous wartime broadcasts. There is even a telephone scrambler system, concealed as a lavatory; this gave the prime minister a hotline to the White House. A museum displays the great man's red velvet romper suit, bowler hat, champagne and cigars.

ST JAMES'S PARK

Now stroll into **St James's Park** ⑪ (www.royalparks.org.uk; daily 5am–midnight; free). Henry VIII first formed it by draining a swamp; Charles II decked it out in French style with a straight canal; and George IV, with architect John Nash, put a bend in the lake, gave it an island and also a bridge with some of the best views in London. Today, the park is a favourite lunching spot for civil servants from nearby government offices – if you are peckish too, consider stopping at **Inn the Park**, see ❶.

THE MALL

Emerging from the park on its northern perimeter, you find yourself on

> ## Big Ben
>
> At the northern end of the Palace of Westminster is the Clock Tower, standing 316ft (96m) tall. It was Pugin's last design before his descent into madness and death. It houses five bells, which strike the Westminster Chimes every quarter hour. The largest of these, which strikes the hour, is Big Ben, the third-heaviest bell in England, weighing 13.76 tonnes. The name 'Big Ben' properly refers only to this bell, but is often used to refer to the whole tower. The huge clock (the faces are 23ft/7m in diameter) is famous for its reliability. It is fine-tuned with a small stack of old penny coins on its pendulum: adding or removing a penny changes the clock's speed by two fifths of a second per day. UK residents can arrange to climb Big Ben – apply to your MP or a member of the House of Lords.

the pink tarmac of The Mall, the processional route running from Aston Webb's **Admiralty Arch** (1912) to his **Queen Victoria Memorial** (1911) in front of Buckingham Palace. The road was originally laid out by Charles II when he wanted a new pitch for *pallemaille* (Pall Mall, his favourite pitch, had become too crowded). This was a popular game of the time, and involved hitting a ball through a hoop at the end of a long alley.

Carlton House Terrace

Almost opposite where Horse Guards Road joins The Mall, is a grand staircase leading up to Nash's **Carlton House Terrace** ⑫. This complex, completed in 1835, was built on the site of the recently demolished mansion of the Prince Regent (later George IV), who had decided to move to a revamped Buckingham House (later Buckingham Palace).

The enormous column in between the two sections of terrace is a tribute to 'The Grand Old Duke of York' of the children's nursery rhyme. The duke was in fact commander-in-chief during the French Revolutionary Wars. The memorial was paid for by stopping a day's pay from all ranks of the army.

ICA

Tucked under Carlton House Terrace on the Mall is the **Institute of Contemporary Arts** ⑬ (www.ica.org.uk; Tue–Sun 11am–11pm; charge), with a gallery, cinema, café-bar and bookshop. It was founded in 1948 by art critic Herbert Read, with a remit to challenge traditional notions of art.

St James's Palace

Walking down The Mall towards Buckingham Palace, on your right you pass the garden walls of **Marlborough House**, built by Christopher Wren from 1709 to 1711. It was the home of Queen Mary, grandmother of the present Queen, until her death in 1953. Adjacent, on Marlborough Road, is the Queen's Chapel, designed by Inigo Jones; its interior can be viewed during Sunday services, from Easter to July.

Next on your right is **St James's Palace** ⑭ (closed to the public). This castellated brick building was commissioned by Henry VIII, but only became the principal residence of the monarch in London from 1698, when Whitehall Palace burnt down. This is where Mary I died, Elizabeth I waited for the Spanish Armada to sail up the channel, and Charles I spent his final night before being executed. It is now the administrative centre of the monarchy.

Close by is **Clarence House** (access from The Mall; www.royalcollection.org.uk; guided tours Aug Mon–Fri 10am–4pm, Sat–Sun 10am–5.30pm; charge), the residence of Prince Charles, and formerly (1953–2002), the home of the Queen Mother, whose art collection and mementoes are still in place.

Buckingham Palace

BUCKINGHAM PALACE

Now, continue to the forecourt of **Buckingham Palace** ⓰ (www.royal collection.org.uk; State Rooms daily late July–Aug, 9.30am–7pm, Sept 9.30am–6pm; buying tickets in advance online strongly advised; charge). Originally the country house of the Duke of Buckingham (hence the name), the building was bought in 1761 by George III for his wife, Queen Charlotte. George IV came to the throne in 1820 and had the mansion transformed into a palace by the architect John Nash. By 1829, however, the costs had risen to £500,000, and Nash was replaced by Edward Blore to finish the work.

On completion, the first monarch to move in was Queen Victoria, in 1837. Remarkably, she soon found there were no nurseries and too few bedrooms, so a fourth wing was built. The palace finally arrived at its present state in 1914, when the facade was redesigned by Sir Aston Webb.

In front of the Palace, Changing the Guard takes place daily, as at Horse Guards (www.changing-the-guard.com; May–July daily at 11.30am; Aug–April alternate days at 11.30am, see website for details; free). Here, the ceremony is accompanied by music from the Guards' band and takes 40 minutes.

The State Rooms

The Palace has 775 rooms, including 52 royal and guest bedrooms, 188 staff bedrooms and 78 bathrooms. In summer, when the Queen stays at Balmoral Castle in Scotland, the State Rooms (used regularly by the Queen for state banquets, receptions and ceremonies) are open to the public. The sumptuous interiors feature paintings by Rembrandt, Vermeer, Poussin and Canaletto, as well as fine sculpture and furniture.

Queen's Gallery

Further along Buckingham Palace Road from the entrance to the State Rooms is the **Queen's Gallery** (daily 10am–5pm; charge). This displays selections from the royal art collection, including numerous royal portraits (notably by Holbein and Van Dyck), paintings by Rembrandt, Rubens and Canaletto, and drawings by Leonardo, Holbein, Raphael, Michelangelo and Poussin.

Food and Drink

① INN THE PARK

Northeast Section of St James's Park; tel: 020-7451 9999; www.peytonand byrne.co.uk; daily B, L, AT and D; self-service area: £–££; formal restaurant: £££

Features kedgeree or a full English for breakfast, and afternoon tea. Self-service snacks also available. Service can be slow.

Botticelli's Venus and Mars

NATIONAL GALLERIES

In a neoclassical building with a 'pepperpot' dome, looking out over Trafalgar Square, is one of the world's finest art collections, displaying about 2,300 masterpieces dating from the mid-13th century to 1900. Adjacent is a gallery devoted to the national collection of portraits.

DISTANCE: 0.15 mile (0.25km) not incl. distance covered in galleries
TIME: Half a day
START: National Gallery
END: National Portrait Gallery

This tour takes in two of London's most important art galleries, and looks at their collections in detail. The walk can easily be combined with route 1.

THE NATIONAL GALLERY

The **National Gallery** ❶ (www.nationalgallery.org.uk; daily 10am–6pm, Fri till 9pm; free) was founded in 1824, when a private collection of 38 paintings was acquired by the British Government for the sum of £57,000 and exhibited in the house of the late owner, banker John Julius Angerstein, at 100

Pall Mall, a modest beginning in contrast with grand institutions such as the Louvre in Paris or Madrid's Prado.

The move to Trafalgar Square

Before long, a more suitable home for the growing collection was sought. The solution came with William Wilkins' long, low construction, opened in 1834 on the then-recently created Trafalgar Square. From the start, however, the building has been criticised as being somewhat inadequate, and additions ever since have done little to confront the shortcomings.

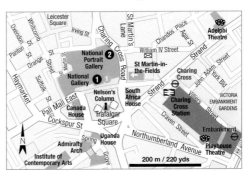

Turner's Fighting Temeraire

The Sainsbury Wing

In 1991 a major extension, the Sainsbury Wing, was built to provide much-needed facilities: new galleries, a lecture theatre, a restaurant, shop and space for temporary exhibitions. It was designed by the postmodern US architect Robert Venturi to harmonise with the rest of the building, while offering a humorous comment on its classical idiom. A previous, more avant-garde proposal had been scrapped after Prince Charles's now-famous denouncement of it as 'a monstrous carbuncle on the face of a much-loved and elegant friend'.

Tour of the collection

The National Gallery's collection is arranged chronologically, from the 13th century to the end of the 19th, through four wings, starting in the Sainsbury Wing, which contains works from the 13th to 15th centuries. Starting here means resisting the temptation to go into the gallery through its grand main entrance (from where a magnificent staircase offers you a choice of three directions), but it makes sense in terms of the chronology.

Highlights here include medieval and earlier Renaissance works, among them Van Eyck's *The Arnolfini Portrait* (1434), Piero della Francesca's *The Baptism of Christ* (1450s) and the jewel-like *Wilton Diptych* (1395–9) by an unknown artist.

Renaissance galleries

From the Sainsbury Wing, take the walkway east towards the main building's West Wing and the Renaissance galleries. Here, rooms 2 to 12 display masterpieces of the 16th century, including Raphael's *The Madonna of the Pinks* (1506–7), purchased in 2004 for £22 million; Titian's *Bacchus and Ariadne* (1520–3); and Michelangelo's unfinished *The Entombment* (1500–1).

North Wing

From either room 9 or 14 (in the West Wing), you can access the North Wing, which houses paintings from 1600 to 1700. Here you will find dramatic works by Caravaggio and Rubens, and pensive self-portraits by Rembrandt. Always worth seeking out are Vermeer's quiet and enigmatic *A Young Woman standing at a Virginal* (c.1670–2) and Velázquez's more exuberant *Rokeby Venus* (1647–51), the Spanish painter's only surviving nude.

East Wing

In the East Wing are paintings advancing the story of art from 1700 right up to the threshold of modernity. From the aristocratic portraits of Gainsborough and the rural backwaters of John Constable's landscapes (including *The Hay Wain* of 1821), you soon find yourself, a few rooms on, confronted by the optical innovations of Seurat's *Bathers at Asnières* (1884), the vibrant colours and violent emotions of Van Gogh's *Sunflowers* (1888) and the hints of Cubism in Cézanne's *Bathers* (c.1894–1905).

After all that, you can now recuperate in the Gallery's excellent café immedi-

National Portrait Gallery

Elizabeth I portrait, the NPG

ately below, on Level 0, see ①. Before you leave, don't forget to see the works by Leonardo in room E (closed until 2014) on the same level, as well as Holbein's *The Ambassadors* (1533) in room C (closed until 2014).

NATIONAL PORTRAIT GALLERY

Tucked behind the National Gallery, to the northeast, on St Martin's Place, is the **National Portrait Gallery ❷** (www. npg.org.uk; daily 10am–6pm, Thu and Fri until 9pm; free except special exhibitions), which is full of famous British faces.

Background

A British historical portrait gallery was founded in 1856, the initiative of the 5th Earl of Stanhope. With no collection as such, it relied on gifts and bequests, the first of which was the 'Chandos' picture of William Shakespeare (c.1610), attributed to John Taylor and probably the only portrait of Britain's most famous playwright done from life.

From the start, additions to the collection (initially comprising traditional paintings, drawings and sculpture, with photography added later) were determined by the status of the sitter and historical importance of the portrait, not by their quality as works of art, criteria that still pertain today. Portraits of living people were not admitted until 1968, when the policy was changed to encourage younger artists and a fresh exploration of the genre.

The collection

The stylish galleries display portraits of important British people past and present. The displays are broadly chronological, starting on the second floor (reached by the vast escalator from the ticket hall) and ending on the ground floor. There are thematic sub-divisions within each period: the Tudors and 17th- and 18th-century portraits on the second floor; the Victorians and 20th-century portraits (to 1990) on the first floor; and, on the ground floor, the ever-popular British portraits since 1990 and (usually) excellent temporary exhibitions.

Highlights include self-portraits by Hogarth and Reynolds, Patrick Branwell Brontë's painting of his literary sisters Charlotte, Emily and Anne, and numerous royal portraits. The contemporary galleries have a curiosity value for seeing how today's celebrities are being recorded for posterity.

Food and Drink

① THE NATIONAL CAFÉ

Ground Floor, National Gallery; tel: 020-7747 5942; www.nationalgallery.org.uk; B, L and D: Mon–Fri 8am–11pm, Sat 9am–11pm, Sun 9am–6pm; ££

Waiter-service brasserie, self-service area and espresso bar. Particularly good breakfasts: eggs Benedict, porridge, French toast, etc. Look out for the crisps that are cooked and bagged to order.

Covent Garden street performer

COVENT GARDEN AND SOHO

East of Charing Cross Road is Covent Garden: once London's fruit and vegetable market, it is now a magnet for shoppers. West of Charing Cross is Soho, which has many excellent restaurants and pubs, as well as a thriving gay scene, Chinatown, plenty of cinemas and lots of sex shops.

DISTANCE: 2 miles (3km)
TIME: A full day
START: Covent Garden tube
END: Leicester Square
POINTS TO NOTE: Note that many shops in central London are open until late on Thursdays (usually until around 8pm), so it may be a good idea to walk the retail-heavy Covent Garden half of this route at that time.

The first half of this walk takes you through the district of Covent Garden. It acquired its name during the reign of King John (1199–1216) as the kitchen garden of Westminster Abbey (or 'Convent') and became a major producer of fruit and vegetables in London for more than three centuries.

In 1540, however, Henry VIII dissolved the country's monasteries, appropriated their land, and formed the Church of England, which, with himself at its head, would be more amenable to his frequent changes of wife. Henry granted Covent Garden to Baron Russell, later the first Earl of Bedford.

In the early 17th century, the fourth Earl of Bedford commissioned Inigo Jones to redevelop the area, creating much of the streetplan you see today, as well as the piazza, colonnades and church. Before long a fruit and vegetable market here was thriving, and over the next 250 years, it became the most important in the country.

By the 1970s, though, the congestion of central London had become too much and the market moved south of the river. The 1980s brought a revival, and the district was reinvented as a shopping, eating and tourist hub. Today, the area is equally renowned for its shopping, bars and nightclubs, and eccentric street entertainers.

COVENT GARDEN

From **Covent Garden tube station** (outside which there are always crowds of people) turn right on to Long Acre, lined with high-street chain stores, and then immediately

Covered market interior　　　　　　　　　　　　　*Neal's Yard*

left on to Neal Street, which is full of fashion-forward boutiques. Here, you can buy designer streetwear, natural shoes, baskets, kites, China tea, chic toiletries, handbags and jewellery and the latest trainers.

Turn left on to Earlham Street, where, on your right at No. 41, is the **Donmar Warehouse** (booking tel: 0844-871 7624; www.donmarware house.com), one of London's most innovative theatres. Continue along Earlham Street to the tiny roundabout known as **Seven Dials ❶**, the junction of seven streets, then turn right on to Shorts Gardens. At Nos 21–3 is an eccentric water-driven clock above the window of a health food shop; and at No. 17 is Neal's Yard Dairy, an excellent cheese shop. This marks the entrance (on the left) to **Neal's Yard ❷**, which is healthfood central – a triangle of shops selling all manner of health foods as well as offering restorative holistic treatments, and with the Wild Food Café for vegetarians and lovers of raw food.

Continue up Shorts Gardens, across Neal Street again, and turn right on to Endell Street. Just nearby you can pick up some old-fashioned British grub at the acclaimed **Rock & Sole Plaice**, see ❶. Further down Endell Street, on your left at no. 24, is **The Hospital Club**, a heavily designed art gallery and members' club created by the pop group Eurythmics' Dave Stewart and Microsoft's Paul Allen.

Royal Opera House

Crossing over Long Acre again, you hit Bow Street, home of the 'Bow Street Runners', the forerunners of the police, and the former Magistrates' Court, where Oscar Wilde was convicted in 1895 for committing 'indecent acts'.

Located directly opposite is the **Royal Opera House ❸** (www.roh.org. uk; free admission to the Floral Hall, charge for backstage tours). Now home to the Royal Opera and Ballet companies, the theatre was founded in 1728 with the profits from *The Beggar's Opera* by John Gay. Since then it has experienced highs and lows, from staging premieres of Handel's operas to being twice burnt down. It is currently riding high after renovation in the 1990s, and, aside from performances, you can now have lunch here, drink in the bar, see exhibitions and take in views of London's skyline from the magnificent Floral Hall.

Covent Garden Market

Walking around the side of the Opera House, down Russell Street, you come to **Covent Garden Market ❹**. Originally the convent garden of Westminster Abbey, the site came into the possession of the earls of Bedford, who commissioned Inigo Jones to design a new residential estate in the 1630s. Houses in the terraces facing the square were set above arcades as in the elegant rue de Rivoli in Paris, and the fruit and vegetable market was

Apple Market, Covent Garden

established here not long afterwards. It continued until 1974, when it was moved to Nine Elms on the South Bank near Vauxhall.

The Covered Market

The market building was redesigned by Charles Fowler in 1830. In the North Hall is the Apple Market, which hosts antiques stalls on Mondays, and arts and crafts from Tuesday to Sunday. Surrounding it are speciality shops such as Pollock's, which sells old-fashioned toy theatres among other amusements. The Punch & Judy pub nearby is a reminder that Punch's Puppet Show was first performed here

in 1662, as witnessed by diarist Samuel Pepys.

London Transport Museum

In the southeast corner of the square is the **London Transport Museum** ❺ (www.ltmuseum.co. uk; daily 10am–6pm, Fri from 11am; charge). This child-friendly museum deals with all aspects of London travel, from vehicles and uniforms to signs and posters. Look out in particular for the A Class steam locomotive which hauled passenger trains on the first London Underground line from 1866 until electrification in 1905. There is a shop on the ground floor selling transport related memorabilia.

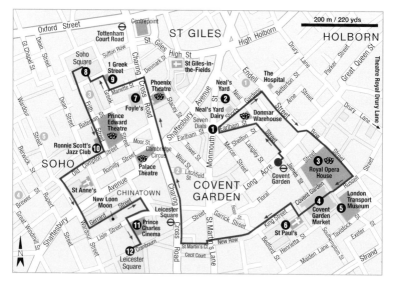

Market stalls

St Paul's Church

On the western side of the square is **St Paul's** (www.actorschurch.org; Mon–Fri 8.30am–5pm, Sun 9am–1pm; free). In 1631, the earl of Bedford commissioned Inigo Jones to build the church, reportedly on a tight budget, prompting the architect's remark, 'You shall have the handsomest barn in England!' Now known as the 'Actors' Church', for its association with the many theatres in the parish, it contains memorials to Charlie Chaplin, Noël Coward, Vivien Leigh and Gracie Fields.

CHARING CROSS ROAD

Walk down King Street, to the right of the church as you face it, and, at the crossroads, continue on to the partly pedestrianised New Row. When you reach St Martin's Lane, it might be worth a detour to the southern end, where the Coliseum is home to English National Opera (ENO; www.eno.org). While performances at the Royal Opera House are sung in the vernacular, here they are in English. Tickets are cheaper than those at Covent Garden, and can sometimes be bought on the night.

Otherwise cross over St Martin's Lane and walk through St Martin's Court. Then turn right on to Charing Cross Road. This major road, linking Trafalgar Square with Tottenham Court Road, is traditionally the preserve of London's booksellers. Many have now been forced out by the high rents, but a few remain, including several antiquarian dealers. Try Cecil Court, the next pedestrianised alley to the south from St Martin's Court, for Hogarth prints, Victorian folding maps of London, vintage theatre posters, modern first editions and sheet music.

Further north on Charing Cross Road is Litchfield Street, on your right, where **Le Beaujolais** is located, see ②. Continuing up past Cambridge Circus, on the left, is **Foyle's** bookshop ⑦ (once the world's largest; it was due to move to premises next door in early 2014). Then just afterwards is Manette Street, named after Charles Dickens' Dr Manette in *A Tale of Two Cities* and a fitting introduction to Soho, where many French émigrés settled after the Revolution.

SOHO

Bounded by Regent Street, Charing Cross Road, Oxford Street and Leicester Square, Soho embodies the myths of both 1960s 'swinging London' and its more recent, 1990s, ironic version, 'cool Britannia'. Although the maze of narrow streets may not quite live up to the promise of either, there is a definite buzz to the district, helped by the presence of part of London's gay and lesbian scene, as well as a cluster of youthful media companies.

Before the 17th century, however, this was all open fields, and used as a hunting ground. The first streets to be

Chinatown

developed were Old Compton, Gerrard, Frith and Greek streets, laid out in the 1670s by bricklayer Richard Frith.

Today these streets are lined with bars, restaurants and clubs, and remain busy almost around the clock. Despite this being one of London's major night-life centres, what you see is still a considerably cleaned-up version of the old louche Soho, although there are still remnants of a red-light district, tucked away on the quieter streets.

Soho Square and Greek Street

Back at Manette Street, where you entered Soho, turn right into Greek Street and walk up to **Soho Square** ❽. A statue of Charles II shares the square with a ventilation shaft heavily disguised as a half-timbered cottage. Most of the 18th-century houses around the square have been surrendered to television, PR and advertising companies, but **No.1 Greek Street** ❾ (www.hosb. org.uk) has been preserved by a charity for the homeless. Even when the house is closed, its cantilevered 'crinoline' staircase and rococo plasterwork can be glimpsed through the windows.

Frith Street

Now head south from Soho Square via Frith Street. At No. 6, the critic and essayist, William Hazlitt (1778–1830), uttered his last words, 'Well, I've had a happy life,' which should please those staying at the hotel now occupying the building. Opposite is **Arbutus**, see ❶,

and, beyond, on the corner of Bateman Street, the Dog and Duck pub, with its exuberant Victorian decoration.

Further down, at No. 21, is the house where the paying public came in 1765 to see the nine-year-old Mozart play, thereby replenishing his father's coffers. Opposite, at No. 18, you can test your own musical abilities at **Karaoke Box** (tel: 020-7494 3878; www.karaokebox. co.uk). A few doors along at No. 22 is **Bar Italia**, which is open till fashionably late, although otherwise remains impervious to trends. This building is where John Logie Baird gave the first public demonstration of television in 1926.

On the other side of the road, at No. 47, is **Ronnie Scott's Jazz Club** ❿ (tel: 020-7439 0747; www.ronniescotts. co.uk), where Count Basie played, Ella Fitzgerald sang, and Jimi Hendrix gave his last public appearance.

Around Old Compton Street

At the end of Frith Street, turn right on to Old Compton Street, the focus of Soho's gay scene. Carry on to the end of Old Compton Street and continue at the crossroads on to Brewer Street and **Randall & Aubin** ❹, which is sandwiched neatly between sex shops and Italian delicatessens.

Chinatown

Back on Wardour Street, a little to the north, is the popular, dependable **Busaba Eathai**, see ❺, while, if you follow the street south, across Shaftesbury

Bar Italia

Old Compton Street

Avenue, there is the **Wong Kei**, at Nos 41–3, an almost comic multi-storey Chinese restaurant, with famously brusque staff and cheap, yet not so cheerful, food.

Turn left soon afterwards on to **Gerrard Street**, which is Chinatown's main thoroughfare. At No. 9 is the **New Loon Moon supermarket**, in an 18th-century purpose-built brothel. Opposite, at No. 43, is the **New Loon Fung supermarket**, once home to the poet John Dryden (1631–1700).

Leicester Square

At the end of Gerrard Street, turn right at Newport Place, then right again into Lisle Street. Turn left at the excellent **Prince Charles Cinema** ⓫ (www.princecharlescinema.com), which puts on beer and pizza nights, singalong events and double bills, on Leicester Place to reach **Leicester Square** ⓬. Here, surrounded by the city's largest cinemas – a frequent venue for film premieres – the route ends.

Food and Drink

① ROCK & SOLE PLAICE

47 Endell Street, Covent Garden; tel: 020-7836 3785; daily L and D; £
London's oldest fish and chip shop (est. 1871). The master-fryer offers the catch of the day (sometimes even mullet or Dover sole). Sit inside or out, and if you like, bring your own wine.

② LE BEAUJOLAIS

25 Litchfield Street; tel: 020-7836 2955; Mon–Sat L & D; ££
Noisy, cramped and chaotic, yet friendly, fun and unpretentious, this wine bar serves French bistro fare (and vegetarian options) to the accompaniment of blues and jazz.

③ ARBUTUS

63–4 Frith Street; tel: 020-7734 4545; www.arbutusrestaurant.co.uk; daily L and D, pre-theatre dinners Mon–Sat from 5pm; ££
Michelin-starred restaurant that offers remarkable value, especially at lunch time. All the wines, no matter how expensive, are available by the glass or carafe. The modern European dishes are imaginative and tasty. Booking essential.

④ RANDALL & AUBIN

16 Brewer Street; tel: 020-7287 4447; www.randallandaubin.com; daily L and D; ££
Named after the old delicatessen that inhabited this spot for 90 years, Randall & Aubin has inherited a feeling of shopping bustle. Piles of lobster, crabs and oysters greet you as you enter.

⑤ BUSABA EATHAI

106–10 Wardour Street; tel: 020-7255 8686; www.busaba.com; daily L and D; ££
Stylishly designed Thai restaurant, with a convivial atmosphere (owing, in part to the communal tables). Serves fresh Thai food at reasonable prices. Good vegetarian options.

Regent Street

PICCADILLY AND MAYFAIR

The heart of the West End presents grand thoroughfares, glorious churches and fine art galleries. But beware: you will need your credit card handy for this route, since it takes in some of London's most exclusive shopping streets.

DISTANCE: 2.25 miles (3.5km)
TIME: Half to a full day
START: Piccadilly Circus
END: Oxford Street
POINTS TO NOTE: If you are a keen shopper, the time scale could extend indefinitely, as you shop between sights.

Not for nothing is Mayfair the most expensive square on the London Monopoly board. This is the area for five-star hotels, art dealers, Bentley showrooms, offices of hedge funds and haute couture stores. Running east–west on its southern edge is Piccadilly (smart St James's is to the south), while Oxford Street, the capital's high street, runs along the north boundary. On the western border is Park Lane (the second most expensive square on the Monopoly board).

Regent Street

Forming the eastern boundary of Mayfair, curving northwards from Piccadilly Circus, is **Regent Street**, Britain's first purpose-built shopping street, designed by John Nash and completed in 1825. It was built to link the future George IV's residence at Carlton House in St James's to Regent's Park, and is still part of the Crown Estate today. Although the present route will take you down Piccadilly itself, worthwhile destinations on Regent Street for another time include the toyshop Hamley's, Art Nouveau Liberty & Co., and the BBC's Broadcasting House, beyond Oxford Street.

PICCADILLY CIRCUS

Coming out of Piccadilly tube station, you enter the melée of **Piccadilly Circus ❶**. Above are the famous neon billboards; the first electric advertisements appeared here in 1910.

The porticoed building on the northeastern side of the circus, the **London Pavilion**, was built as a music hall in 1859; sadly today it is a rather uninspiring shopping centre. On the south side is the more appealing **Criterion Theatre**, designed by Thomas Verity and

The Eros statue   *Hamley's worker*

opened in 1874; after refurbishment, it is once again putting on plays.

Eros

In the centre of the circus is a fountain topped with a statue known as **Eros**. It was erected in 1892–3 to commemorate Lord Shaftesbury, a Victorian politician who campaigned for better conditions in factories and coal mines, for mental health provision and child welfare. Despite its name, the aluminium statue is actually of Eros's twin, Anteros. The sculptor Alfred Gilbert chose Anteros as the embodiment of selfless love, using a 16-year-old Italian boy as his model.

Piccadilly

Leaving Piccadilly Circus, walk along Piccadilly. The street's name is thought to have come from 'piccadill', the stiff collars you see in portraits of Elizabeth I or Sir Walter Raleigh, and made by a 17th-century local tailor, Robert Baker. On the south side of the street, in a fine Art Deco building, is the flagship branch of Waterstone's, supposedly the largest bookshop in Europe.

St James Piccadilly

A little further down is the church of **St James Piccadilly** ❷ (www.sjp.org.uk; daily; free), designed by Christopher Wren and consecrated in 1684. Seek

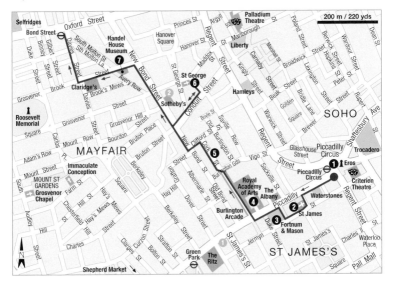

Fortnum & Mason

out the carved work of Grinling Gibbons: the fine limewood reredos and the marble font (in which the poet William Blake was baptised).

Shopping

Directly behind the church is **Jermyn Street**, lined with London's finest shirtmakers and gentlemen's outfitters. Take a look there before returning to Piccadilly, where the next stretch of the road offers other interesting shopping opportunities. At No. 187 is the bookshop **Hatchard's**, which has operated on this site since 1801. The young Noël Coward was caught shoplifting here in 1917, packing books into a stolen suitcase. A few doors down is **Fortnum & Mason ❸**, grocers to the royal family. Even if you do not want to buy anything it is worth popping in to see its beautifully preserved Edwardian interior. Further along again is another gorgeous interior, this time a restaurant, the **Wolseley ❶**, open for refreshment at any time of day.

Royal Academy of Arts

On the opposite side of Piccadilly is Burlington House, home of the **Royal Academy of Arts ❹** (www.royalacademy.org. uk; daily 10am–6pm, Fri until 10pm; charge), founded in 1768. A statue of its first president, the painter Joshua Reynolds, can be seen in the front courtyard. The Academy's main function today is the staging of large exhibitions of great art from the past. There is also an annual summer exhibition of new art, to which anyone can submit pictures for inclusion; the best are selected and are available for purchase.

From the Royal Academy, walk through Burlington Arcade, just adjacent on the west side. Watch out for the 'Beadles', guards who patrol this haven of luxury boutiques in their traditional uniforms of top hats and tailcoats.

MAYFAIR

Emerging from the arcade you will find yourself on Burlington Gardens, in Mayfair. Off to the right is Savile Row, where bespoke tailors create the finest men's suits in the world, while to the left are the fashion emporia of exclusive Bond Street. Immediately in front of you, however, is Cork Street.

Commercial Art Galleries

Cork Street ❺ is one of the places in London (others include Dover Street, Dering Street and Bond Street, all nearby) where the top art dealers cluster. Major galleries on this street include Bernard Jacobson at No. 6 and Waddington Custot at Nos. 11–12. Among the most successful artists represented here are Frank Stella, Robert Indiana, Peter Blake, Ben Nicholson and Jack B. Yeats.

Bond Street

At the end of Cork Street turn left on to **Bond Street**, where you will find exclu-

Burlington Arcade *Selfridges interior*

sive couturiers and designer boutiques (Chanel, Gucci, Prada, et al), jewellers (Asprey, Boucheron, Bulgari), as well as art and antiques galleries. The southern half of the street is the more upmarket. At Nos. 34–5 is the headquarters of **Sotheby's**, the famous auctioneers founded in 1744. Members of the public are free to enter and watch an auction or view the items for sale. There is also an excellent café, see ②.

Walking north up Bond Street, a short detour off to the right on Maddox Street brings you to **St George's Church** ❻ (www.stgeorgeshanoversquare.org; Mon–Fri 8am–4pm, Sun 8am–noon; free). When it was first built, George Frederick Handel was a regular worshipper here; much later, it was the venue for the weddings of George Eliot (1880) and Teddy Roosevelt (1886).

Brook Street
Back on Bond Street, further up and off to the left is Brook Street. At No. 25, among more luxury goods shops, is the **Handel House Museum** ❼ (www.handelhouse.org; Mon–Sat 10am–6pm, Sun noon–6pm; charge), where the composer of *The Messiah* lived from 1723 until his death in 1759. Next door, much later (1968–9), lived a very different musician – Jimi Hendrix – commemorated by a blue plaque.

Further up Brook Street you will come to **Claridge's**, one of the city's smartest hotels.

Oxford Street
Turning north up Davies Street (opposite Claridge's) you emerge on **Oxford Street**, where, as well as souvenir shops, there are big department stores – notably Selfridges, John Lewis and House of Fraser. When you have had enough shopping, escape via one of the tube stations: going from west to east, Marble Arch, Bond Street, Oxford Circus or Tottenham Court Road.

Food and Drink

❶ THE WOLSELEY
160 Piccadilly; tel: 020-7499 6996; www.thewolseley.com; daily B, L, AT and D; £££
This place was built as a car showroom in 1921, converted into a posh branch of Barclay's Bank in 1927, then a restaurant in 2003. The interior is exceptional, and the breakfasts (including omelette Arnold Bennett – made with haddock, mustard and cheese), all-day menu for snacks (even steak tartare) and afternoon tea (nice cakes) are delicious. Lunch and dinner are also good, but booking is advisable.

❷ SOTHEBY'S CAFÉ
34–5 New Bond Street; tel: 020-7293 5077; www.sothebys.com; B, L and AT; ££
For a reasonable-value breakfast, lunch and afternoon tea in an expensive neighbourhood, bear in mind the surprisingly unstuffy café on the ground floor of this venerable auction house.

The Wallace Collection

MARYLEBONE

In contrast to hectic, overtly commercial Oxford Street to the south, elegant Marylebone exudes a calm villagey air. This walk takes you along its main artery, with art, waxworks and Victorian sleuthing along the way.

> **DISTANCE:** 1.25 miles (2km)
> **TIME:** Half a day
> **START:** Bond Street tube
> **END:** Baker Street
> **POINTS TO NOTE:** Visit Madame Tussauds after 5pm to reduce the price and queuing time.

The need to relieve congestion in Oxford Street in the early 18th century inspired the building of a new road from Paddington to Islington through the parish of St Mary-by-the-bourne. The wealthy Portman family funded the development of the adjacent district: Marylebone (pronounced 'marry-le-bun'), which retains its genteel ambience and many of its Georgian buildings.

ST CHRISTOPHER'S PLACE

From **Bond Street** tube, cross to the other side of Oxford Street and walk north up narrow **St Christopher's Place** ❶, a pedestrian enclave full of boutiques and cafés.

North of St Christopher's Place is Wigmore Street, where medical specialists spill over from nearby Harley and Wimpole streets, the domains of private physicians since the 1840s.

WALLACE COLLECTION

Turn left on Wigmore Street, then second right on to Duke Street, which leads to Manchester Square. On the far side of the square is Hertford House and the **Wallace Collection** ❷ (www.wallacecollection.org; daily 10am–5pm; free).

Bequeathed to the British nation by the widow of Richard Wallace, the illegitimate son of the fourth Marquess of Hertford, the collection comprises paintings, furniture, porcelain and armour. Highlights include works by Boucher, Fragonard, Watteau, Franz Hals (notably his *Laughing Cavalier*), Rembrandt and Rubens. The gallery has a restaurant.

THE HIGH STREET

Turn left as you leave the gallery and take Hinde Street east off the square.

St Christopher's Place   Sherlock Holmes Museum

Turn left at the crossroads and walk up Thayer Street, which becomes **Marylebone High Street 3**. This strip has the feel of a well-heeled urban village, with chic boutiques, bookstores (the Oxfam Bookshop and Daunt Books), gourmet delicatessens and hip cafés.

Halfway up, on the left, is Moxon Street and **La Fromagerie**, see ❶; on Sunday a farmers' market is held here (10am–2pm). Back on the high street, at No. 55, is the Conran Shop, occupying a former stables.

MARYLEBONE ROAD

At the top of Marylebone High Street is the east–west artery, **Marylebone Road**. Straight ahead is the **Royal Academy of Music 4** (www.ram.ac.uk; museum: Mon–Fri 11.30am–5.30pm, Sat noon–4pm; free), which hosts concerts and is home to a museum of historic instruments and archive material.

Opposite is **St Marylebone 5**, the fourth church on this site. Walk west at this point for **Madame Tussauds 6** (www.madame-tussauds.co.uk; usually daily July–Sept 9am–5.30pm, Oct–June 10am–5.30pm but check website; charge). Expect to queue for a while before seeing the wax and silicone doppelgängers.

BAKER STREET

Now continue further west for Baker Street. At No. 239 is the **Sherlock Holmes Museum 7** (www.sherlock-holmes.co.uk; daily 9.30am–6pm; charge), which recreates the home of Sir Arthur Conan Doyle's fictional supersleuth.

Fountain in the Inner Circle

REGENT'S PARK

The extravagance of the Prince Regent led to the founding of Regent's Park, worth visiting for its rose gardens, boating lake and zoo, and Regent Street, which linked the park to his old home on The Mall.

DISTANCE: 2.5 miles (4km)
TIME: Half to a full day
START: Regent's Park tube
END: London Zoo
POINTS TO NOTE: Consider taking the canal boat here from Camden Lock.

Regent's Park (www.royalparks.org.uk; daily 5am–dusk; free) was originally part of Henry VIII's hunting chase around London. It began to take on its current form in 1811, when the Prince Regent (1762–1830), the future George IV, took control and hired John Nash as architect. Of Nash's original scheme, not everything was realised: his summer palace was never built, and only eight of 56 villas for the Prince's friends were erected (two survive); however, his terraces, churches, barracks and river were all put in place.

The park became home to the Zoological, Royal Toxophilite (archery) and Royal Botanic societies, and opened to the public in 1835. A century later Queen Mary's Gardens were added.

NASH'S TERRACES

Emerging from **Regent's Park tube station** at the centre point of Nash's Park Crescent, fortify yourself with breakfast or lunch at the **RIBA Café**, see ❶ (Portland Place is due south and on the left). Walk back up again and cross the busy road to Park Square East, where formerly you would have entered the **Diorama ❶**, a three-storey glass-roofed auditorium. At the square's northeast corner is St Andrew's Place, dominated by the Royal College of Physicians, the arch-modern masterpiece – completed in 1964 – of architect Denys Lasdun.

Food and Drink

❶ RIBA CAFÉ

66 Portland Place; tel: 020-7850 5533; daily B, L and D; ££
Stylish 1930s setting in the headquarters of the Royal Institute of British Architects. Fresh, light meals.

London Zoo *Birds on the boating lake*

Walk up the Outer Circle past **Cambridge Gate ②**, built in 1880 on the site of the Colosseum – a domed building that housed a canvas panorama of London, demolished in 1875.

Next along is patrician Chester Terrace: walk through the middle of this via **Chester Gate ③**. To the right of the archway is a small villa and, mounted on the wall, a bust of Nash. Emerging from the archway at the end of the terrace, turn left and cross over the Outer Circle to enter the park.

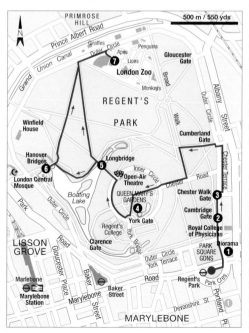

QUEEN MARY'S GARDENS

Follow the path straight on into the park until you reach **Broad Walk**, lined with benches. Turn left, then right on Chester Road, for the **Inner Circle** and **Queen Mary's Gardens ④**, with 400 varieties of roses, and water gardens, and, on the far side, a café and the open-air theatre (www.openair theatre.org).

THE LAKE

Rejoining the Inner Circle at York Gate, walk clockwise round to the path for **Longbridge ⑤**, which leads over the lake. Follow the path along the far side of the lake to the **Hanover Bridges ⑥**, where boats can be hired (Apr–Sept 10am–6pm; charge).

LONDON ZOO

To visit **London Zoo ⑦** (www.zsl.org; Mar–Oct daily 10am–5.30pm, until later in July–early Sept, Oct–Feb daily 10am–4pm; charge), take a path north from either Longbridge or the Hanover Bridges. At the Outer Circle turn right for the zoo's main entrance.

BLOOMSBURY

This is the intellectual part of town. There's the vast British Museum, the homes of Charles Dickens, Virginia Woolf and other literary luminaries, the University of London and a museum of Egyptian archaeology.

DISTANCE: 2 miles (3km)

TIME: A full day

START: British Museum

END: Russell Square

POINTS TO NOTE: The nearest tube station to the British Museum is Tottenham Court Road. To reach the starting point from there, leave the tube station via the exit for the Dominion Theatre, walk north up Tottenham Court Road, then turn right into Great Russell Street. Just after the crossroads with Bloomsbury Street, the British Museum is on your left. The museum is vast, so allow at least half a day to explore it.

Bloomsbury is bounded to the north by Euston, St Pancras and King's Cross railway termini, but this is no typical station hinterland. It is the hotbed of London's intellectual activity: it was home to the Bloomsbury literati of the early 20th century, and still has a distinctly cultural and academic atmosphere, as it is where both the British Museum and the University of London are sited.

BRITISH MUSEUM

The **British Museum** ❶ (www.british museum.org; daily 10am–5.30pm, Fri until 8.30pm; free; short tours of selected exhibits, 30–40 minutes, available daily, free) is one of the oldest museums in the world, founded by an Act of Parliament in 1753 and opened in 1759. It has accumulated a collection of 8 million objects. Devote just 60 seconds to each and you would be there for more than 15 years.

Although only 50,000 objects are on display, this is not a place to rush through in an hour. It is also one of the most visited attractions in London and the best time to go is soon after opening. As there are so many things to see, we cover the highlights below, so that you can prioritise, according to your interest.

Note that options for refreshments in or near the museum include the museum cafe in the Great Court, redesigned by architect Norman Foster. Alternatively, head for **Truckles**, see ❶, by leaving the museum, then turning left, crossing over and taking a right turn

Egyptian mummies

on to Bury Place; Truckles is in a court-yard just on your left.

Egyptian Mummies: Rooms 62–3

By far the biggest crowd-puller in the museum are the Egyptian sarcophagi. Thanks to enthusiastic plundering by 19th-century explorers, the collection (located on the upper floor) is the richest outside Egypt.

Rosetta Stone: Room 4

Another major attraction is the 2nd-century BC granite tablet known as the Rosetta Stone, which provided the key for deciphering Egyptian hieroglyphics. In the same room is the colossal sandstone head of pharaoh Rameses II, said to be the inspiration for *Ozymandias*, Shelley's poem on the transience of power.

Elgin Marbles: Room 18

Among the museum's more controversial holdings are the Elgin Marbles, which represent the high point of ancient Greek art. Carved in the 5th century BC, they depict the battle of the Lapiths and Centaurs, a festival procession for the Goddess Athena, as well as various Greek gods.

The marbles were taken from the Parthenon temple on the Acropolis in Athens by Lord Elgin in the early 19th century. His action, ironically, saved them for posterity, since the acropolis temples were employed for storing munitions during the Greek War of Independence (1821–33) and much of what remained was reduced to ruin. Understandably, the Greeks want the sculptures returned.

Benin Bronzes: Room 25

In the basement are around five dozen of the 900 brass plaques found in Benin City, Nigeria, in 1897. The Benin Bronzes were probably cast in the 16th century to clad the wooden pillars of the palace; they depict court life and ritual in extraordinary detail.

Anglo-Saxon Ship Burial: Room 41

The Sutton Hoo Ship Burial was the richest treasure ever dug from British

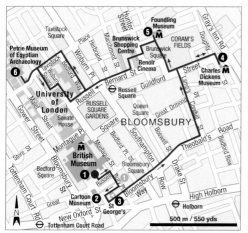

Cartoon Museum

soil. The early 7th-century longboat was probably the burial chamber of Raedwald, an East Anglian king. The acidic sand had destroyed all organic material well before the excavation in 1939, but a rich hoard of weapons, armour, coins, bowls and jewellery survived.

Other highlights

In room 40 are the Lewis Chessmen, found on the Isle of Lewis in Scotland's Outer Hebrides and probably made in Norway. These 12th-century chess pieces are elaborately carved from walrus ivory and whales' teeth. The helmeted figures and faces set in curious scowls are almost comical.

Room 50 exhibits the preserved corpse of Lindow Man, the victim of a sacrifice, who was found in a peat bog in Cheshire in 1984. Scientists were able to determine his blood group, what he looked like and what he had eaten.

HISTORIC STREETS

When you are finished at the museum, walk down Bury Place and turn right at Little Russell Street. Follow this road across Museum Street to stop at the **Cartoon Museum** ❷ (www.cartoonmuseum. org; Mon–Sat 10.30am–5.30pm, Sun noon–5.30pm; charge) on your right at No. 35. Alternatively, browse in the bookshops and galleries on Museum Street before continuing the route by turning left on to Bloomsbury Way at the bottom of the street.

Almost immediately on your left is the church of **St George's Bloomsbury** ❸ (www.stgeorgesbloomsbury.org. uk; Mon 1–4pm, Tue–Fri 1–2pm, Sat 11.30am–5pm, Sun 2–5pm; free), the sixth and final London church designed by Nicholas Hawksmoor, the leading architect of the English Baroque. Completed in 1731, it has a steeple in the form of a stepped pyramid surmounted by Britain's only statue of George I.

Continuing along Bloomsbury Way, cross over Southampton Row to Theobald's Road. The fifth turning on your left is Lamb's Conduit Street, full of shops, historic pubs, cafés and restaurants. Continue to the end of the street, then turn right at Guildford Place and right again on to Doughty Street.

DICKENS MUSEUM

At 48 Doughty Street is the **Charles Dickens Museum** ❹ (www.dickensmuseum. com; daily 10am–5pm; charge). The author lived here from 1837–9 while writing *Nicholas Nickleby and Oliver Twist*. It is the only one of his London homes still standing, and exhibits all manner of memorabilia: his letters, manuscripts, desk, locks of his hair and even his lemon squeezer.

FOUNDLING MUSEUM

Retrace your steps to Guildford Place, where, on your right, is **Coram's Fields**, a children's park (adults admitted only

The Brunswick Centre   *Pub on Lamb's Conduit Street*

with a child). Facing on to the park on the west side at 40 Brunswick Square is the **Foundling Museum ❺** (www.foundling museum.org.uk; Tue–Sat 10am–5pm, Sun 11am–5pm; charge). Formerly Thomas Coram's Foundling Hospital, it cared for 27,000 abandoned children between 1739 and 1953, when it closed.

As well as telling the hospital's story – with poignant mementoes left by mothers for their babies – the museum has important collections relating to two of its first governors, the artist William Hogarth and the composer George Frederick Handel. Hogarth encouraged artists of the day to donate works and, in doing so, created Britain's first public art gallery. The collection includes works by Hogarth, Reynolds and Gainsborough, displayed in the original interiors.

Handel donated proceeds from annual performances of *The Messiah* and bequeathed the manuscripts to the hospital. The museum has since acquired a huge collection relating to Handel, including manuscripts, books and music, libretti and paintings.

UNIVERSITY OF LONDON

Leaving the Foundling Museum, head for the other side of the square and the Futurist-inspired Brunswick Centre, designed by Patrick Hodgkinson in 1973 and given a much-needed face-lift in 2006. Walk up the steps by the Renoir arts cinema and turn left through the complex past the cafés and restaurants to emerge on Bernard Street. Walk past the tube station and on to Russell Square. Turn right off the square on Bedford Way and you are in university territory.

At the end of the street, turn left and walk along the south side of Gordon Square. Blue plaques on the houses here commemorate the residences of various members of the Bloomsbury Group. Economist J.M. Keynes lived at No. 46 and Lytton Strachey at No. 51. Continuing west of the square on to Byng Place, look out on your right for Malet Place, an inconspicuous lane that leads into University College and the **Petrie Museum of Egyptian Archaeology ❻** (www.petrie.ucl.ac.uk; Tue–Sat 1–5pm; free). Inside, look for the world's oldest dress (2800BC).

Finally, return to Russell Square by turning right off Gordon Square, cutting through Woburn Square and turning left.

Food and Drink

❶ TRUCKLES

Pied Bull Yard, off Bury Place; tel: 020-7404 5338; www.davy.co.uk/truckles; Mon–Fri L and D; ££

Traditional Ale and Port House in a courtyard next to the London Review of Books Bookshop. Simple and modern upstairs; candle-lit tables and sawdust-covered floors downstairs; seating outside in summer. Dishes include dressed crab, lamb shank and treacle tart.

Temple Bar

HOLBORN AND THE INNS OF COURT

This area is the domain of journalists and lawyers so vividly described in the novels of Charles Dickens. The atmosphere is well preserved in the winding backstreets, rickety old pubs, quaint shops and historic churches.

DISTANCE: 2 miles (3km)
TIME: Half to a full day
START: St Bride's, Fleet Street
END: Somerset House
POINTS TO NOTE: The walk may take a whole day if you visit all the museums on the route.

This tour starts at the western end of Fleet Street, a strip synonymous with print journalism, although the industry has long since moved out. To continue where many a hack left off, set yourself up for the tour with a stop at the **Blackfriar**, one of the many historic watering holes in this part of London, opposite Blackfriars Station. When sated, walk north to Ludgate Circus, then turn left on to Fleet Street to follow the bank of the old Fleet River, which is now buried in a sewer.

FLEET STREET

On the left, down Bride Lane, rises the steeple of **St Bride's** ❶ (www.stbrides. com; Mon–Fri 9am–6pm, Sat times vary, Sun 10am–6.30pm; free). This

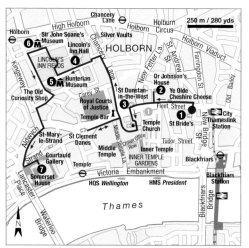

church, the inspiration for the first tiered wedding cake, was built by architect Sir Christopher Wren after the Great Fire of London destroyed its medieval predecessor in 1666. Unfortunately, the church was gutted again during the Blitz in 1940, though it has been carefully restored. A museum in the crypt displays Roman mosaics, Saxon church walls as well as a product of England's first printing press, William Caxton's *Ovid*.

Offices of national newspapers

On the other side of Fleet Street are the former offices of Britain's national newspapers, which relocated in the 1980s to cheaper, high-tech sites such as Wapping in the Docklands. At No. 121 is an Art Deco building of black glass and chromium (nicknamed Black Lubyanka), which was once the nerve-centre of Express Newspapers. A few doors down, the pillared palace at No. 135 used to house *The Telegraph*.

Dr Johnson's House

On the same side of the road, look out for **Ye Olde Cheshire Cheese** pub (rebuilt 1667), once frequented by Samuel Johnson and his cronies, including Oliver Goldsmith, who lived at No.6. From here it is just a short, well-signposted, walk to **Dr Johnson's House** ❷ on Gough Square (www.drjohnsonshouse. org; Mon–Sat 11am–5.30pm, until 5pm in winter; charge). Johnson lived here from 1748 to 1759, compiling his dictionary in the garret with six poor copyists. Outside the house is a statue of Johnson's pet cat, Hodge – 'a very fine cat indeed'.

Returning to Fleet Street, cross the road to **El Vino**, see ❶.

Church of St Dunstan-in-the-West

On the other side of Fleet Street, just beyond Fetter Lane, is **St Dunstan-in-the-West** ❸ (www.stdunstaninthewest. org; Mon–Fri 9.30am–5pm; free). It is famous for its 17th-century clock (its two giants strike the hours and quarters), and its association with poet-priest John Donne, who was rector here (1624–31). Over the porch at the side is a statue of Queen Elizabeth I, the only one known to have been carved during her lifetime.

THE INNS OF COURT

Further along, on the left at No. 17, is the **Inner Temple Gateway**, leading to the quadrangles, chambers and gardens of one of the four Inns of Court. Enter the lane beneath and continue to **Temple Church**, part of which was built in the 1180s for the Knights Templar. Head left across Church Court to King's Bench Walk (where Tony Blair once practised as a barrister) and turn right. Soon, turn right again on to Crown Office Row, and continue past the gardens (Mon–Fri 12.30–3pm; free) to emerge on Middle Temple Lane.

Turn right, passing on your left the buildings of another of the Inns of Court, **Middle Temple**, and you come out at the

Lincoln's Inn

point where Fleet Street ends and the Strand begins. This, the boundary of the City of London, is marked by **Temple Bar**, a stone monument topped with a dragon. Further west (in the middle of the road) is the church of **St Clement Danes**, built in 1682 by Sir Christopher Wren. It was damaged in the Blitz but then restored as the church of the Royal Air Force.

Chancery Lane

On the far side of the road are the **Royal Courts of Justice**, where England's most important civil law cases are heard. To its right is Chancery Lane. As you walk up, on your left is Carey Street where you can find the Silver Mousetrap jewellers (est. 1690) and the **Seven Stars** pub, the 'Magpie and Stump' of Dickens's *Pickwick Papers*.

Lincoln's Inn Fields

Further up Chancery Lane, enter **Lincoln's Inn** ❹ through the arch on the left marked 'New Square'. The more aptly named Old Hall was built during the reign of Henry VII (1485–1509). Walk straight through to the east gate and

Lincoln's Inn Fields, London's largest square. On the south side the Royal College of Surgeons houses the **Hunterian Museum** ❺ (www.rcseng.ac.uk; Tue–Sat 10am–5pm; free) with a collection of fine art, as well as anatomical specimens.

Sir John Soane's Museum

On the north side of the square at No. 13 is the eccentric **Sir John Soane's Museum** ❻ (www.soane.org; Tue–Sat 10am–5pm and first Tue of month 6–9pm; free). Soane (1753–1826), best known as the architect of the Bank of England, designed this, his own house. Its rooms are just as he left them: packed with antiquities and paintings, including Hogarth's *Rake's Progress* and *The Election*.

Leave the square by the southwest corner, on Portsmouth Street. **The Old Curiosity Shop** from Dickens's novel is on the left (now selling shoes). Navigate the lanes south to reach Aldwych, which leads back to the Strand.

SOMERSET HOUSE

On the south side **Somerset House** ❼, a Palladian mansion built by Sir William Chambers from 1776–96, is home to the **Courtauld Gallery** (www.courtauld. ac.uk; daily 10am–6pm; charge, Mon tickets half price), displaying outstanding paintings, from Michelangelo to Monet. In summer, the fountains in the courtyard make way for open-air cinema, while in winter there is an ice rink.

Tower of London

THE CITY

Despite its rich history, the City is no museum. Hi-tech office towers crowd the dome of St Paul's Cathedral, and the Beefeaters at the Tower of London are vastly outnumbered by 300,000 business suits on their daily commute.

DISTANCE: 2.25 miles (3.5km)
TIME: A full day
START: Tower of London
END: Smithfield Market
POINTS TO NOTE: Walk this route on a weekday, as the City is dormant at weekends.

The nearest tube to the starting point is Tower Hill. From the tube exit turn right towards the Tower of London. As you walk down the steps of the subway, a section of the old Roman city wall is on your left. On the other side of the road, turn right; the main entrance to the Tower is on the river side.

TOWER OF LONDON

It was in 1078 that William the Conqueror ordered the building of the **Tower of London** ❶ (www.hrp.org.uk; Tue–Sat 9am–5.30pm, Sun–Mon 10am–5.30pm; charge). Since then, the most haunted building in England has housed a zoo (from the reign of King John, 1199–1216), a palace (under Henry III, 1216–72) and a VIP prison (inmates included Elizabeth I, Guy Fawkes, Walter Raleigh and briefly, in 1941, Rudolf Hess).

To see the Tower, you might join one of the hour-long tours led by a Yeoman Warder (a Beefeater). Visit the **White Tower**, the only intact Norman keep left in England, and the armoury, which contains an execution axe and chopping block (two of Henry VIII's wives were beheaded here). See also the **Crown Jewels**, stored here since 1303. As well as crowns, orbs and sceptres, there is a 2m (6.5ft) wide punchbowl. Outside, watch out for the Royal Ravens: legend has it that if they ever leave, the Tower will crumble. This came close to happening in World War II, when all but one died from shock during bombing raids.

ALONG THE RIVER

If you are now in need of a rest, cross over Tower Bridge Approach on the eastern side of the Tower of London

St Paul's Cathedral

to **St Katharine's Dock** ❷, where you can enjoy a drink at one of the cafés overlooking the marina. Here, Telford's fine warehouses, once piled with ivory tusks, are the backdrop for Thames barges, restored clippers and an 18th-century warship, *The Grand Turk*.

Now, returning to the main entrance of the Tower, walk up Lower Thames Street, passing **Custom House** (1817) on your left, followed by **Old Billingsgate Market**, which for centuries had supplied London with fish. Further along, again on the left, is Sir Christopher Wren's church of **St Magnus the Martyr** ❸, completed in 1676. It marks the entrance to the original London Bridge, which stood until 1831. There is a model in the vestibule.

THE MONUMENT

Just before the bridge, turn right up Fish Street Hill to **The Monument** ❹ (www.themonument.info; daily 9.30am–6pm, until 5.30pm in winter; charge), a memorial to the Great Fire of 1666, which started in a bakery on Pudding Lane, just nearby. Built by Christopher Wren and Robert Hooke in 1671–7, this 61m (202ft) Doric column was designed to double as a scientific instrument, with a central shaft for use as a zenith telescope (a hinged lid in the flaming urn at the top covers the opening). Around this shaft wind 311 steps leading up to a cage (added after several suicides) from where you can admire the view.

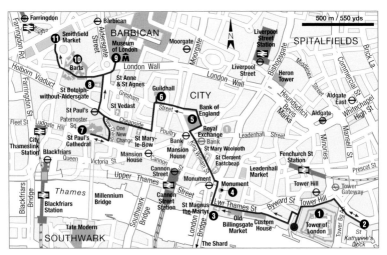

Side door, Bank of England

The Gherkin

BANK OF ENGLAND

At the top of Fish Hill Street turn left, and, after the major junction, bear right up King William Street into the financial heart of the City. On the way, you pass Wren's church of **St Clement Eastcheap** on your right (of the nursery rhyme, *Oranges and Lemons*), then Nicholas Hawksmoor's **St Mary Woolnoth**, also on the right. At the end of the street, as you approach the Bank of England, on your left is **Mansion House** and on the right is the **Royal Exchange**, and Cornhill, leading east to **Simpson's Tavern**, see ❶.

On the far side of the junction is Britain's central bank, the **Bank of England** ❺ (www.bankofengland.co.uk; Mon–Fri 10am–5pm; free). Designed by architect Sir John Soane in 1788, the building has more space below ground than is contained in the 42 storeys of Tower 42 on Old Broad Street, the City's tallest building.

Just around the corner on Bartholomew Lane is a **museum** (Mon–Fri 10am–5pm; free) displaying banknotes, gold bars (you can even pick one up), minting machines and examples of firearms that were once issued to bank branches for defence.

THE GUILDHALL

At the top of Bartholomew Lane, turn left on Lothbury and continue until you reach the City of London's town hall, the

Guildhall ❻ (www.cityoflondon.gov.uk; phone for times; free). Built from 1411 on the site of a Roman amphitheatre (the outline of the arena is marked in black on the courtyard), this is the only secular stone building to have survived the Great Fire of 1666. Inside is a large medieval hall with stained glass and extensive crypts.

To the rear is the **Guildhall Library** (Mon–Sat 9.30am–5pm; free), founded in the 1420s with a bequest from Richard Whittington, three times City mayor, and later the inspiration for the pantomime character, Dick. As well as a reference library specialising in London history, it houses the museum of the City Clockmakers' Company, displaying more than 600 timepieces.

On the right of the square is the **Guildhall Art Gallery** (Mon–Sat 10am–5pm, Sun noon–4pm; charge). The collection includes Britain's largest painting, *The Siege of Gibraltar* by John Singleton Copley, and Victorian masterpieces by artists such as Millais and Landseer.

ST PAUL'S CATHEDRAL

Now walk down King Street, opposite the Guildhall, and turn on to Cheapside. Coming up on your left is the first of three Wren churches, **St Mary-le-Bow**. Tradition has it that to be a true cockney (East London's old working class), you have to be born within earshot of the sound of the bells. Further along, on your right, is the church of **St Vedast**.

Museum of London exhibit

Then, on your left, down New Change, is **St Paul's Cathedral** ❼ (www.stpauls.co.uk; Mon–Sat 8.30am–4pm; charge).

Pristine white after years of renovation, the cathedral (the fifth on this site) was completed in 1708, on Wren's 76th birthday, after its predecessor was gutted in the Great Fire of 1666. In the later stages of its building, Wren is said to have hauled up to the rafters in a basket to inspect progress. Inspired by St Peter's Basilica in Rome, the building is centred under a dome rising 108m (354ft) from the floor.

The dome holds three circular galleries. First, up 259 steps, is the Whispering Gallery running around the inside of the dome: whisper against its wall at any point, and your voice is audible to a listener with their ear held to the wall at any other point around the gallery. Oddly, speak at a normal volume, and the sound does not transmit in the same way. The ceiling is decorated with monochrome paintings by Sir James Thornhill of scenes from the life of St Paul. The other two galleries are both outside: the Stone Gallery is 378 steps from ground level, and the Golden Gallery, 530 steps up.

If heights are not your forte, visit the crypt. Christopher Wren was the first to be interred here, in 1723 at the age of 90. Other famous names include the Duke of Wellington and Lord Nelson, the latter having been brought back from the Battle of Trafalgar preserved in a barrel of French brandy.

POSTMAN'S PARK

Return now to New Change, head north, and after the crossroads continue on to St Martin's Le Grand, which then becomes Aldersgate Street. On your right is Wren's unusual brick church of **St Anne and St Agnes**, based on the plan of a Greek cross.

Opposite, by the church of **St Botolph-without-Aldersgate** (built by George Dance the Elder in 1725) is the **Postman's Park** ❽, the brainchild of painter and philanthropist George Frederick Watts (1817–1904). It was originally a popular lunch time spot for workers from the former General Post Office, nearby. It is now noted for its wall covered in Doulton plaques commemorating fatal acts of bravery by the ordinary people of the Victorian era.

MUSEUM OF LONDON

Further up Aldersgate Street, past the busy roundabout, is the **Museum of London** ❾ (www.museumoflondon.org.uk; daily 10am–6pm; free). This museum takes you from London's earliest beginnings right up to the late 20th century. Highlights include Roman leather 'bikinis', Viking battle-axes, a hoard of Tudor jewellery, dress and costume, from royal gowns to Norman Hartnell 1920s flapper dresses, paintings by artists from Canaletto to Henry Moore, and the Lord Mayor's gilded coach. There is also a large audiovisual exhibit

The Barbican   *The museum at Barts*

on the Great Fire, as well as a walk-through Victorian street scene.

BARTS HOSPITAL

From the museum, cross to the other side of the roundabout and walk up Montague Street. Turn right on to Little Britain to the complex of **Barts** ❿. When you emerge on West Smithfield, turn left for the Henry VIII Gate and the historic part of the hospital. Founded in 1123, Barts is the oldest surviving hospital in England – though all that remains of its medieval fabric is on your left as you enter: the 15th-century chapel of St Bartholomew-the-Less. Walk through the first courtyard for the main square's North Wing, built by James Gibbs in the 1730s. It

contains the Baroque **Great Hall** and the **Museum** (www.bartshealth.nhs.uk; Tue–Fri 10am–4pm; free), which offers a history of the hospital as well as access to two spectacular murals (1736–7) by William Hogarth, who used real patients as some of his models.

SMITHFIELD MARKET

On the other side of West Smithfield is **Smithfield Market** ⓫, where livestock and meat have been traded since the 10th century. At various times the site has also been used for jousting, public executions (notably William Wallace's in 1305), the selling of wives and for Bartholomew Fair, which, from 1133 to 1855, drew crowds to its cloth market and pleasure fair. Today, the place is occupied by Sir Horace Jones's market buildings, built from 1866 above railway lines linking farmers and butchers across the country. The pubs around the market open famously early.

The Barbican

To the northeast of the Museum of London is the Barbican, a complex comprising 2,000 flats (in London's tallest residential towers) as well as a theatre, concert hall, cinema, art gallery, library, school, YMCA, fire station and even an ornamental lake. It was built between 1965 and 1976 on a 35-acre (14-hectare) site. Despite numerous design problems – wind moans through the walkways, it is easy to get lost, the concrete was the wrong type and requires constant maintenance – it is still Britain's finest example of concrete Brutalist architecture.

Food and Drink

● SIMPSON'S TAVERN

Ball Court, 38 Cornhill; tel: 020-7626 9985; www.simpsonstavern.co.uk; Mon–Fri B and L; ££

Down an alley off Cornhill, this time-warped tavern has served hearty pies and stews and puddings (with custard) to old-school-tie-wearing City gents since 1759.

South Bank skateboarders

THE SOUTH BANK

A riverside walk along the south bank of the Thames takes in some of the city's most important cultural institutions, as well as Shakespeare's London and the fashionable area around Borough Market.

DISTANCE: 2 miles (3.5km)
TIME: Half to a full day
START: County Hall
END: HMS Belfast
POINTS TO NOTE: Do the walk on Friday or Saturday to see Borough Market in full swing.

The nearest tube station to the starting point is Waterloo. From here, leave by the overhead walkway signposted 'Southbank Centre', and as you descend the steps, you cannot miss the big wheel of the London Eye in front of you.

COUNTY HALL

Start at **County Hall ❶**, on your left as you reach the Eye. This huge Edwardian building was the seat of the Greater London Council until it was controversially disbanded by Margaret Thatcher in 1986. Now privately owned, it contains two hotels, an aquarium, an art gallery, games arcade and several restaurants.

Namco Station (www.namcofunscape. com; 10am–midnight; charge), has bumper cars, video games, karaoke and a bowling alley. Close by is the entrance to the **London Aquarium** (www.visitsea life.com; daily 10am–7pm, until 8pm school holidays; charge). Some 350 species are represented, but the high-

Book market by the BFI

The South Bank by night

light is the sharks. There is also a pool where you can touch some of the inhabitants. Feeding time for rainforest species, including piranhas, is Mon, Wed and Fri 1pm; for sharks, Tue, Thu and Sat 2.30pm.

County Hall is also home to the **London Dungeon** ❷ (www.thedungeons. com; Mon–Fri 10am–5pm, from 11am Thu, Sat–Sun 10am–6pm, opens until 7pm in school holidays; charge). Lasting about 1.5 hours, a tour led by actors features ghoulish exhibits on the Black Death, the Great Fire of 1666 and Jack the Ripper's exploits, as well as several ghost-train-style rides. It is fun for children who like the macabre, but the visit is spent in darkened corridors, so

it is not recommended for those under eight. Note that queues can be long and tickets are expensive.

LONDON EYE

Next stop is the **London Eye** ❸ (www.lon doneye.com; daily Apr–Aug 10am–9pm, Sept–Mar 10am–8.30pm; charge), the world's largest observation wheel, designed by husband-and-wife architects David Marks and Julia Barfield.

The 32 enclosed capsules take 30 minutes to make a full rotation, which is slow enough to let passengers step in and out of the capsules while the wheel is moving. On a clear day, you can see for 25 miles (40km). Book ahead if you

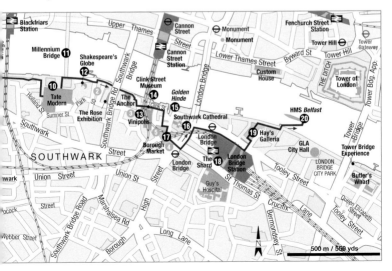

Fountain at Queen Elizabeth Hall

want to ride at busy periods, and do check the weather forecast first.

SOUTHBANK CENTRE

Now continue along the riverside walk to the concrete bulk of the **Southbank Centre** ❹ (www.southbankcentre.co.uk). The largest arts complex in Europe, it regularly puts on free entertainment, from lunch-time gigs and 'Commuter Jazz' (Fri 5.45–7pm) to talks on poetry and art. It is fronted by a row of restaurants (including Giraffe – a good choice if you have children), and a bookshop.

Music Venues

The **Royal Festival Hall** is a legacy of the 1951 Festival of Britain, intended to improve Londoners' morale after the austerity of the post-war years. In 2007, a major renovation of the hall was completed, giving it improved acoustics, better foyer facilities and two new restaurants: Skylon, with views of the river, and, around the back, the ground-floor **Canteen**, see ❶.

Next door are the 917-seat **Queen Elizabeth Hall** for music, dance and public lectures, and the 372-seat **Purcell Room**, for recitals of classical chamber music and world music.

Hayward Gallery

Adjacent, on the upper level of the Southbank Centre complex, is the **Hayward Gallery** (Mon noon–6pm, Tue–Wed, Sat–Sun 10am–6pm, Thu–Fri 10am–8pm; charge), one of London's most important venues for contemporary art exhibitions.

BFI Southbank

Next to the Hayward is Britain's leading arthouse cinema, **BFI Southbank** ❺ (tel: 020-7928 3232; www.bfi.org.uk). With three auditoria and an intimate studio cinema, it holds more than 2,400 screenings and events every year, from talks by film stars to silent movies with live accompaniment. The cinema also houses a research area, a shop, and an excellent 'Mediathèque', where visitors can browse the British Film Institute's archive for free (call ahead to reserve). For a drink before a screening, try the everpopular Riverfront café in front of the building, with tables and benches sheltering under Waterloo Bridge, or, for more plush surroundings, visit the upstairs **Benugo Bar & Kitchen**.

The **BFI** also runs **London Imax** ❻, a 5-minute walk away in the centre of the roundabout at the southern end of Waterloo Bridge. This cylindrical, glass building houses Britain's largest cinema screen, together with steeply raked seating.

NATIONAL THEATRE

Just to the east of the Southbank complex is the **National Theatre** ❼ (www.nationaltheatre.org.uk). Built to designs by Sir Denys Lasdun and opened in 1976, this concrete behemoth houses three theatres: the 1,200-seat Olivier,

On the Millennium Bridge

Shakespeare's Globe

the 900-seat Lyttelton and the Dorf-man, a more intimate space due to open in spring 2014 with galleries on three sides. For a peek behind the scenes, book a one-hour 15 minute backstage tour (see website for times; charge).

OXO TOWER

After the theatres, you pass **Gabriel's Wharf** ❽, with restaurants and gift shops, and, close by, the Art Deco **OXO Tower** ❾. Architect Albert Moore had grand ideas for this project: as well as erecting what was to become London's second highest commercial building, he wanted to use electric lights to spell out the product's name. When planning permission was refused because of an advertising ban, Moore came up with the idea of using three letters – O, X and O – as windows looking out north, south, east and west. Inside the tower are several smart restaurants; it's a glamorous, and expensive, spot for cocktails with stunning river views.

TATE MODERN

To the east of Blackfriars Bridge lies the former colossal Bankside Power Station, which is now **Tate Modern** ❿, home to the Tate's international contemporary art collection (covered in detail in route 11).

In front of Tate Modern is the graceful **Millennium Bridge** ⓫, a pedestrian link to St Paul's Cathedral (see route 9).

Unveiled in 2000, it was the first new river crossing over the Thames in central London since Tower Bridge in 1894. However, on its opening day, crowds on the bridge caused it to sway alarmingly, and it had to close for structural amendments by its architect, Norman (now Lord) Foster. By 2002, the wobble was fixed, and it reopened.

SHAKESPEARE'S GLOBE

Heading a little further east, you reach Bankside, one of the South Bank's most historic areas. The district grew up in competition with the City opposite, but by the 16th century had become a den of vice, famous for brothels, bear- and bull-baiting pits, prize-fights and the first playhouses, including the Globe.

A replica of the original (1599) open-air Globe Theatre, called **Shakespeare's Globe** ⓬, opened here in 1996 after years of fund-raising. The thatched roof was the first permitted in London since the Great Fire of 1666. **Shakespeare's Globe Exhibition** (www.shakespeares-globe.com; May–Sept daily 9am–noon, Oct–Apr daily 9am–5pm; charge), to the right of the theatre, fills in the background on the area's historic past. Just opposite is **Tas Pide**, see ❷, a good place for a spot of lunch.

BANK END AND CLINK STREET

At Bank End is the Anchor pub, where little has changed in 200 years. Across

The Shard

the street, in the vaults under the railway viaduct, is **Vinopolis** ⓭ (www.vinopolis.co.uk; wine tasting tours Wed 6–9.30pm, Thu–Fri 2–10pm, Sat noon–9.30pm, Sun 1–5pm; charge), which has a huge wine shop and smart restaurant, see ③.

The Clink

On **Clink Street** are the fragments of the Bishop of Winchester's 13th-century residence, from which the bishops operated a prison. The phrase 'in the clink', a euphemism for being in jail, is thought to stem from the sound made by clanking chains. The **Clink Street Museum** ⓭ (www.clink.co.uk; July–Sept daily 10am–9pm, Oct–June Mon–Fri 10am–6pm, Sat–Sun 10am–7.30pm; charge) recalls the area's gruesome past.

The Golden Hinde

At the far end of Clink Street is St Mary Overy Dock, where parishioners were once able to land goods free of toll and have their wives put in the ducking stool. A gleaming replica of Sir Francis Drake's diminutive ship the *Golden Hinde* ⓯ (www.goldenhinde.co.uk; daily 10am–5.30pm; charge) now sits in the dock.

SOUTHWARK CATHEDRAL

Follow the road round to the right then bear left to **Southwark Cathedral** ⓰ (www.southwark.anglican.org; daily 8am–6pm; free). Shakespeare was a parishioner here, and a memorial in the south aisle shows him reclining in front of a frieze showing Bankside during the 16thcentury. John Harvard, who gave his name to the American university, was baptised here, and is commemorated in the Harvard Chapel. Organ recitals are held in the cathedral on Monday at 1pm and classical concerts on Tuesday at 3.15pm (both free). The refectory is a cosy place for refreshment.

BOROUGH MARKET

In the shelter of the cathedral is **Borough Market** ⓱, a food market dating back to the 13th century. On Thursday, Friday and Saturday the market sells gourmet and organic products. As well as fruit, vegetables, bread and cheese, you will find stalls specialising in game, fish, cakes, preserves, ecologically sound produce, wines and beers, with lots of opportunities to sample the produce. Many stalls do takeaway food, from venison burgers to scallops pan-fried while you wait. **Tapas Brindisa**, see ④, and **Roast**, see ⑤, are two excellent options for lunch.

TOWARDS TOWER BRIDGE

To the east of the market is London Bridge Station and the newly built **Shard** ⓲, Europe's tallest building at

Borough Market sign   *HMS Belfast*

310m (1,016ft). It is a mix of residential and office space, and includes a restaurant and 5-star hotel. You can take a lift to the 72nd floor for unobstructed views of the city and beyond (www.theview fromtheshard.com; book in advance; charge). You can finish the tour here, but if you still have some energy, continue east on Tooley Street to **Hay's Galleria** ⑲, an old wharf now filled in and home to a smart atrium of shops and restaurants.

Continuing through to the riverside, you cannot miss the World War II cruiser **HMS Belfast** ⑳ (www.iwm.org. uk; daily Mar–Oct 10am–6pm, Nov–Feb 10am–5pm; charge). A highlight is immersing yourself in a battle in the Gun Turret Experience.

If you continue east you reach Tower Bridge, where you could cross the bridge to link up with route 9. Alternatively, return to London Bridge for the tube or mainline train.

Food and Drink

① CANTEEN
Royal Festival Hall; tel: 0845-686 1122; www.canteen.co.uk; daily B, L and D; ££
Situated at the back of the Festival Hall, it serves good-quality modern British food in a sleek white interior as well as on the heated terrace outside.

② TAS PIDE
20–2 New Globe Walk; tel: 020-7928 3300; www.tasrestaurants.co.uk; daily L and D; ££
A wide choice of *meze*, as well as *pide* (Turkish pizza), grilled sardines and lamb kofta. Branches also in Borough High Street (tel: 020-7403 7200), near London Bridge, and The Cut (tel: 020-7926 2111), near Waterloo.

③ VINOPOLIS
1 Bank End; tel: 020-7940 8333; www.cantinavinopolis.co.uk; Mon–Sat L and D; ££
Cavernous wine vaults accommodate a restaurant serving good modern British food and, not surprisingly, an exceptional wine list.

④ TAPAS BRINDISA
18–20 Southwark Street; tel: 020-7357 8880; www.brindisa.com; Mon–Sat B, L, D, Sun L and D; £££
Usually packed thanks to its authentic tapas and a buzzing ambience. The only downside is that they do not take reservations.

⑤ ROAST
Floral Hall, Stoney Street; tel: 020-7940 1300; www.roast-restaurant.com; Mon–Sat B, L, D, Sun set meal only 11.30am–6.30pm; ££££
Delicious British food includes succulent organic Banham chicken and sturdy game pies. Breakfasts are scrumptious and reasonably priced.

Tate Modern

TATE TO TATE

Visit Tate Modern, one of London's top tourist attractions and one of the world's most innovative modern art museums, then speed up the river by catamaran to Tate Britain for a survey of British art through the centuries.

> **DISTANCE:** 2.25 miles (3.5km) not including distance in galleries
> **TIME:** A full day
> **START:** Tate Modern, Southwark
> **END:** Tate Britain, Pimlico
> **POINTS TO NOTE:** If you book your boat trip on arrival at Tate Modern, you can enjoy the morning at Bankside, take the boat to Pimlico, have lunch, then spend the afternoon at Tate Britain. Both galleries offer good food and drink options. Alternatively, combine this route with route 10, covering the South Bank.

There are now two Tate galleries in London, and two outside, in Liverpool and St Ives.

The original foundation for the gallery was laid by Henry Tate (who made a fortune by inventing the sugar lump); it opened in 1897 as a department of the National Gallery. The collection now also encompasses the national holdings of international modern and contemporary art.

TATE MODERN

The route begins on the south bank of the river at **Tate Modern** ❶ (www. tate.org.uk; Sun–Thu 10am–6pm, Fri–Sat 10am–10pm; free). The nearest tube stations are London Bridge or Southwark (south of the river) and Blackfriars (to the north), all about 10 minutes' walk away. The lamp-posts between Southwark tube station and the gallery are painted orange to show visitors the way.

The building
In 1998, the Tate made the bold decision to purchase the disused Bankside Power Station, and Swiss architects Herzog & de Meuron won the competition to transform it into an art gallery. The industrial character of Sir Giles Gilbert Scott's original brick structure (built in two stages between 1947 and 1963) was retained. They saved the vast Turbine Hall for housing large-scale art installations, reopened the block's monumental windows and fitted a light at the top of the huge central chimney.

The Turbine Hall

Viewing the Tate Modern collection

A new building is being added to the south of the Tate which will create new galleries and more public space. Work is expected to be completed by 2016, but the main gallery remains open.

The collection

In order to make the permanent collection more accessible to, and more popular with, the general public, the works are ordered by theme. Note that the displays change from time to time.

The permanent collection is hung in four suites, over three floors. On level 2 is 'Poetry and Dream', where the focus is on Surrealist artists and their associates. A large central room (Room 2) includes works by Joan Miró, Picasso, Giacometti, Max Ernst, Salvador Dalí, Francis Bacon, Joseph Beuys and Giorgio de Chirico. 'Transformed Visions' is on level 3, exploring abstract art and its influences. This is where you'll find Mark Rothco's Seagram Murals, paintings which were originally commissioned for the Four Seasons Restaurant in Manhattan but which Rothco eventually decided to give to the Tate.

On level 4 are 'Energy and Process' and 'Structure and Clarity', with the former showcasing artists, such as the Italian Arte Povera movement of the 1960s and '70s, who are interested in transformation and natural forces. 'Structure and Clarity' explores the development of abstract art since the early 20th century, including Cubism, Futurism and Vorticism, with work by Georges Braque, Paul Cézanne, Fernand Léger, Roy Lichtenstein, Auguste Rodin, Henri Matisse and Bridget Riley.

Make sure you see what's going on in the Turbine Hall. This vast hall is five storeys tall, with 37,000 sq ft (3,400 sq m) of floor space, and is used for specially commissioned work by

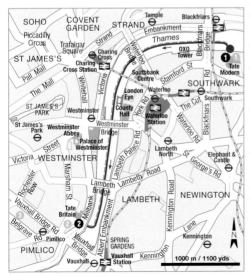

contemporary artists. In 2007, Doris Salcedo created Shibboleth, consisting of a crack running through the concrete floor, while in 2010, Ai Weiwei covered the floor with 100 million hand-painted porcelain sunflower seeds.

There is a restaurant on level 7, see 🛈.

Turner bequest

On his death in 1851, London-born Joseph Mallord William Turner (1775–1851) left a large sum of money and his collection of 20,000 paintings and drawings to the British nation, expressing the wish that a special gallery be built to house them all together. It took until 1987 for this to happen, when the Clore Gallery, designed by British architect James Stirling, was opened beside Tate Britain. Even now, however, some of his paintings are scattered across other collections, contrary to his wishes. Masterpieces on display include *Peace – Burial at Sea*, showing the artist's mastery in depicting light as affected by objects, rather than the other way round, and *Snow Storm: Steam-Boat off a Harbour's Mouth,* suggestive of Turner's fascination with the elemental forces of nature. In order to paint the sensational effect achieved in the latter, Turner tells us in his subtitle that 'The Author was in this Storm on the Night the *Ariel* left Harwich', lashed, at his own request, to the ship's mast.

TATE BOAT

The **Tate Boat** runs every 40 minutes during gallery opening hours, shuttling back and forth between Tate Britain and Tate Modern, and stopping off at the London Eye along the way.

Tickets are available from Tate Modern and Tate Britain, as well as online and by calling 020-7887 8888, or, subject to availability, on the boat itself.

Embarking from the small pier in front of Tate Modern, you are taken in the 220-seat catamaran (with exterior and interior designs by artist Damien Hirst) to Millbank pier in front of Tate Britain. The pier was designed by architects David Marks and Julia Barfield, who were also responsible for the London Eye. It features a lighting installation by artist Angela Bulloch, who was shortlisted for the 1997 Turner Prize. Fluorescent tubing embedded into the floor of the pontoon is computer programmed to provide changing lighting effects at night.

TATE BRITAIN

Tate Britain ❷ (Millbank; www.tate.org.uk; daily 10am–6pm, until 10pm selected Fri; free) in Pimlico is the original Tate Gallery and home to the national collection of British art from 1500 to the present day. Opened in 1897, it was designed by Sydney Smith in classical style, and built on the site of a prison.

The permanent collection is almost entirely contained on one floor (level 2).

Inside Tate Britain

As you enter the building through the front porticoed entrance on Millbank, you go through a succession of grand halls with galleries off to the left and right.

The collection

The galleries within Tate Britain are arranged by date and theme. The only criticism is that there isn't enough space: the majority of the collection has to be kept in storage out of the public view. A much-needed extension is being considered.

Among the British paintings are portraits by William Hogarth (1697–1764) and Thomas Gainsborough (1727–88), views of the English countryside by John Constable (1776–1837) and, in the Clore Gallery, seascapes and landscapes by J.M.W. Turner (1775–1851). Turner bequeathed the paintings to the nation on his death, with the stipulation that they should all be hung in one place, and should be available for the public to see, without charge.

The most popular 19th-century painters represented are the Pre-Raphaelites, including Millais, Holman Hunt, Rosetti and Burne-Jones. Modern British artists represented include Stanley Spencer, Francis Bacon and David Hockney. Sculptures include works by Jacob Epstein, Barbara Hepworth and Henry Moore. The Tate also stages free lectures and film shows, and has a reputation for the avant-garde, with the award of an annual Turner Prize.

When you have finished your survey of British art, retire to the restaurant downstairs, see ❷, or else head for the dependable **Grumbles**, see ❸, just off Belgrave Road to the north of Pimlico tube station.

Food and Drink

❶ TATE MODERN RESTAURANT

Level 6, Tate Modern, Bankside; tel: 020-7887 8888; www.tate.org.uk; Sun–Thu L, AT, Fri–Sat L, AT and D; £££

Wonderful views of London, pleasant hubbub and a style-conscious crowd. Fresh Cornish fish is a speciality. The Level 2 Café, by the ground-floor bookshop, is an alternative, and cheaper, lunch option.

❷ REX WHISTLER RESTAURANT

Tate Britain, Pimlico; tel: 020-7887 8825; www.tate.org.uk; Mon–Fri L and AT, Sat–Sun B, L and AT; £££

The gallery's main restaurant, notable for its mural fantasy, *The Expedition in Pursuit of Rare Meats* (1927) by Rex Whistler, serves stylish contemporary British food. Save room for the white chocolate and rhubarb trifle with champagne jelly, and the cheeses from Neal's Yard.

❸ GRUMBLES

35 Churton Street, Pimlico; tel: 020-7834 0149; www.grumblesrestaurant.co.uk; daily L and D; ££.

Cosy neighbourhood bistro with good-value set-price menus at lunch and early evening (6–7pm). Sunday roast.

HYDE PARK

On May Day 1660, Samuel Pepys wrote in his diary, 'It being a very pleasant day I wished myself in Hyde Park.' Three and a half centuries later, in the heart of a much-changed London, people still feel exactly the same way.

DISTANCE: 2.25 miles (4.5km)
TIME: Half a day
START: Apsley House
END: Queensway tube
POINTS TO NOTE: People with restricted mobility can book a free electric buggy, driven by a volunteer (tel: 07767-498096; www.liberty drives.org.uk; May–Oct Mon–Fri 10am–4pm). Consider doing the route mid-morning to see the Household Cavalry leave their barracks.

Hyde Park was first opened to the public in 1637 by Charles I. It had previously been a deer park used by Henry VIII for hunting and, before that, a manor owned by Westminster Abbey since before the Norman Conquest.

The adjacent Kensington Gardens were sectioned off as the grounds of Kensington Palace in 1689, when William III moved here from Whitehall Palace. Today, all 625 acres (253 hectares) of the park are once again open to the public.

APSLEY HOUSE

The route begins at **Apsley House** ❶ (www.english-heritage.org.uk; closed until April 2014 for refurbishment; charge), near Exit 1 of Hyde Park Corner tube station. Once known as No. 1 London, since it was the first house encountered after passing the tollgates of Knightsbridge, this was where the Duke of Wellington lived from 1817 until his death in 1852. Part of the house is still home to his descendants today.

The house was designed by the architect Robert Adam, and was built between 1771 and 1778. On its passing to the Duke of Wellington, the house had its original brick exterior faced with stone, and the portico and columns were added. Inside, however, much of the original Adam design survives, including the staircase, drawing room and portico room.

Following the Duke's victory at Waterloo, gratitude was heaped upon him in the form of plate and porcelain, paintings, sculpture and chandeliers. The art collection includes works by Goya, Rubens, Correggio and Brueghel. One

Enjoying Hyde Park

gift he should perhaps have refused is an 11ft (3.4m) high nude statue of Napoleon that dominates the stairwell.

HYDE PARK

Enter **Hyde Park** ❷ (www.royalparks. org.uk; daily 5am–midnight; free) via the **Triumphal Screen** to the left of Apsley House. This monumental entrance was commissioned from Decimus Burton by King George IV in the 1820s along with the Wellington Arch, which was later moved to the middle of the roundabout.

If you are fortunate to be here in mid-morning, you might wait at this point to see the Household Cavalry who emerge from their barracks at 10.30am every morning (9.30am on Sunday) on South Carriage Drive and ride across the park to Horse Guards Parade for the changing of the guard. The other road (unmetalled) running east–west and converging on Hyde Park Corner is **Rotten Row** – a corruption of Route du Roi – the king's route from Kensington Palace to Westminster. It was the first road in England to be lit at night – by 300 oil lamps. The Crystal Palace, the spectacular iron-and-glass showcase of the 1851 Great Exhibition, once stood between the two roads. (It was later moved to Sydenham Hill, in southeast London, but burnt down in 1936.)

The Serpentine

Now take the Serpentine Road north-west, past the bandstand on your right, and the rose gardens on your left, to the northern bank of the **Serpentine** ❸. This lake was created by Queen Caroline in 1730 by damming the river

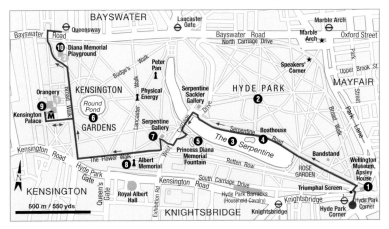

The Orangery

Westbourne. It achieved notoriety in December 1816 when the pregnant wife of the poet Shelley committed suicide by plunging into the icy waters; Shelley married Mary Wollstonecraft Godwin two weeks later. Today, the lake has its own swimming club and is the scene of a famous Christmas Day 100-yard race (www.serpentinelido.com). At the **Boathouse** ❹ you can hire rowing boats and pedalos (Mar–Oct), or take a trip on the solar-powered ferry.

A little further on, West Carriage Drive marks the boundary between Hyde Park and Kensington Gardens. Turn left, and just before the bridge is the **Powder Magazine**. This was originally used for storing gunpowder, but from 2012 it becomes an annexe of the Serpentine Gallery (see below).

To the left of the road on the other side of the bridge is the **Princess Diana Memorial Fountain** ❺, designed by American architect Kathryn Gustafson. This innovative fountain has been dogged by controversy since opening in 2004, owing to the initial cost (£3.6m), and the heavy burdens of ongoing maintenance and supervision. However, it's a popular spot, and children love paddling in its shallow waters.

KENSINGTON GARDENS

Cross over West Carriage Drive and you enter **Kensington Gardens** ❻ (www.royalparks.org.uk; daily 6am–dusk; free). You might have been denied the pleasure of access had Queen Caroline (wife of George II) had her way. On enquiring of Prime Minister Walpole what the cost might be of reclaiming the, by then, public gardens for her private use, she received the reply, 'Only a Crown, Madam'.

Serpentine Gallery

Follow the path off the road for the **Serpentine Gallery** ❼ (www.serpentinegallery.org; daily 10am–6pm; free). This classical-style 1934 tea pavilion puts on major exhibitions of modern and contemporary art. Every spring, a leading architect (Daniel Libeskind, Rem Koolhaas, *et al*), is commissioned to build a temporary pavilion (June–Oct) alongside it.

Albert Memorial

Now follow the signposts along the southwesterly path for the **Albert Memorial** ❽, commissioned by Queen Victoria in memory of her beloved husband, Prince Albert, who died of typhoid in 1861. This Gothic-revival monument was designed by Sir George Gilbert Scott and unveiled in 1872. It centres around a gilded Albert holding a catalogue of the Great Exhibition of 1851. He is surrounded by massive representations of the continents and sits enshrined in a white marble frieze depicting 187 poets and painters. The 180ft (55m) spire is inlaid with semi-precious stones.

Across the road to the south is the **Royal Albert Hall** (www.royalalberthall.com), opened in 1871, and now the

The Albert Memorial   *Kensington Palace gardens*

venue for concerts, including the Proms every summer.

Kensington Palace

Next, to reach **Kensington Palace ⑨** (www.hrp.org.uk; daily Mar–Oct 10am–6pm, Nov–Feb 10am–5pm; charge), continue west, and take a path off to your right in a northwesterly direction. The house came into royal hands in 1689, when William III bought it in the hope that the country air would alleviate his asthma. Additions were made at this time by Sir Christopher Wren, and later by William Kent for George I. Since then it has been inhabited by various members of the Royal Family, most notably Princess Diana, who lived here until her death in 1997; and currently by Prince William and the Duchess of Cambridge.

Highlights inside include Fashion Rules, an exhibition running until summer 2015, featuring dresses from the collections of the Queen, Princess Diana and Princess Margaret. Also impressive is the King's Staircase, with wall paintings of George I's court by William Kent: look out for the king's Polish page Ulric, the Turkish servants Mahomet and Mustapha, Peter 'the wild boy' – a feral child found in the woods in Germany – and a portrait of the artist himself, with his mistress at his shoulder, looking down from the ceiling.

The palace gardens

Outside again, just to the east, near the path by which you entered, is the sunken Dutch garden, and on the other side of the path, a statue of Queen Victoria sculpted by her daughter, Princess Louise, to celebrate 50 years of her mother's reign.

To the north is Hawksmoor's **Orangery**, where Queen Anne liked to take tea, and you can too, see ①. Beyond that is the **Diana, Princess of Wales Memorial Playground ⑩**, where children can make up for having been so well behaved in the tearoom. And when they are tired of clambering over the huge pirate ship at the playground's centre, there is another café for ice creams and cakes, see ②.

Finally, in the northwest corner of the park, leave by the Orme Square Gate, which after 5pm (4pm in winter) is the only exit open. On Bayswater Road, turn right for Queensway tube.

Food and Drink

① THE ORANGERY

Kensington Gardens; tel: 020-7166 6113; daily B, L and AT 10am–6pm, till 5pm in winter; ££
Light lunches and afternoon tea. Outside seating in summer.

② BROADWALK CAFÉ

Kensington Gardens; tel: 020-7034 0722; daily summer B, L and D, 8am–8pm, winter B and L 10am–4pm; £
Ideal for children. Serves salads, pizzas, fruit, yoghurts, ice creams.

V&A exterior detail

SOUTH KENSINGTON
AND KNIGHTSBRIDGE

Museums of decorative arts, natural history and science – the Victorians' rich legacy – are the improving highlights of this tour, after which you can make a less edifying, but equally enjoyable, visit to Harrods.

> **DISTANCE:** 1.25 miles (2km) not including distance covered in museums
> **TIME:** A full day
> **START:** South Kensington tube
> **END:** Knightsbridge
> **POINTS TO NOTE:** All three museums are vast, and visiting all of them in one day would be exhausting; concentrate on one or two, according to interest. Entrance is, however, free, meaning that popping in to see one or two prize exhibits in each is perfectly feasible.

The year 1851 is remembered in Britain for the Great Exhibition, held in Hyde Park in a glass-and-metal palace designed by Joseph Paxton. Aspects of the far-flung Victorian Empire were brought under the curious gaze of a public whose interest in the sciences and the arts had seemingly never been greater. The idea for the exhibition came from Henry Cole (1808–82), chairman of the Society of Arts, and was taken up enthusiastically by the royal consort Prince Albert, who chaired the committee to see it through. Housed in a 'Crystal Palace' built in the park, the event attracted more than 6 million visitors. Afterwards, the building was moved to Sydenham, southeast London, and the exhibition's huge profits were used to purchase 87 acres (35 hectares) in South Kensington to build a more permanent home for the arts and sciences. This area is the focal point of this tour.

V&A

Start at **South Kensington tube station**. Take the underpass in the tube station signposted 'Museums', which brings you out on to Cromwell Road, beside the **Victoria and Albert Museum ❶** (www. vam.ac.uk; daily 10am–5.45pm, Fri until 10pm; free).

The foyer

The museum is vast, with around 5 million objects in its collection, stored in about 8 miles (13km) of galleries. Start in the main foyer, where you can admire the Venetian-inspired 'chandelier' by

Inside the V&A   *V&A exhibit*

American artist Dale Chihuly. The spectacular accretion of blue, green and yellow glass was erected in 1999 as a talking-point for the Victorian foyer, and was doubled in size in 2001 to a height of (33ft) 10m. It was assembled *in situ* by a team of technicians, each piece of glass slotted over an angled rod.

Lower ground and ground floors

On the ground floor, the first galleries on either side of the entrance hall and gift shop display the Asian collections, with treasures from China, Japan, India and the Middle East. Highlights include spectacular rugs and carpets, and the extraordinary *Tipu's Tiger*, a carved automaton of an Indian tiger killing a British officer, made *c.*1790 for Sultan Tipu.

To the far left of the entrance (in room 48a) are the vast *Raphael Cartoons* (1515–16), on loan from the Queen. These drawings, depict scenes from the lives of St Peter and St Paul, and were commissioned by Pope Leo X as templates for a series of tapestries in the Sistine Chapel. Nearby, in room 40, is the revamped fashion gallery.

Flanking the great courtyard are the **Sculpture Courts**, which display masterpieces from around the world. To the rear of the courtyard, near the Ceramic Staircase (which symbolises the symbiotic relationship between art and science), are the three original refreshment rooms, where first-, second- and third-class menus were served prior to World War II. Allusions to food and drink are worked into the decoration. The room by Arts and Crafts pioneers William Morris, Philip Webb and Edward Burne-Jones is particularly fine.

Upper floors

Upstairs, most galleries focus on materials or techniques, such as silver, ironwork (home to Sir George Gilbert Scott's intricate 1862 Hereford Screen), stained glass, ceramics (most of the top floor), textiles and jewellery. The **British Galler-**

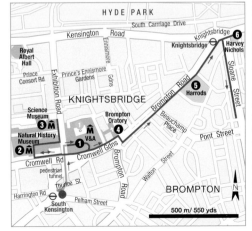

Science Museum

ies, charting British taste from 1500 to 1900, are in rooms 52–8.

Henry Cole Wing

The last remaining section is the Henry Cole Wing, spread over six floors and devoted mostly to changing exhibitions of prints, drawings, paintings and photographs. Also here is the **Frank Lloyd Wright Room**, transplanted here from Pittsburgh, and the only example of the architect's work in Europe. End the tour here with a visit to the museum's café, see ❶.

NATURAL HISTORY MUSEUM

Across Exhibition Road is the neo-Gothic **Natural History Museum** ❷ (www.nhm.ac.uk; daily 10am–5.50pm; until 10.30pm last Fri of month; free). The collection was originally a department of the British Museum, but by the middle of the 19th century it had expanded and outgrown the available space, and in 1881 the present museum opened; it now houses around 75 million plants, animals, fossils, rocks and minerals.

Life Galleries

The first half of the museum is classed as the 'Life Galleries', although ironically its chief attractions – the dinosaurs – are well and truly dead. Just past the information desks, in the middle of the Central Hall, is the cast of a diplodocus unearthed in Wyoming in 1899. At 85ft (26m), it is the longest complete dinosaur skeleton ever discovered.

The **Dinosaur Gallery** is one of the busiest sections of the museum, and many visitors make a bee-line for the robotic dinosaurs at the far end. The full-scale animatronic **T-Rex** on long-term loan from Japan is responsive to human movement; the roaring, life-like model twists and turns, delighting most children (and frightening some).

Human Biology examines the workings behind the human body, from hormones to genes, and is packed with interactive exhibits that will test your memory or trick your senses with optical illusions.

The spectacular suspension of a life-sized blue whale model is the highlight of the **Mammals** section. As well as displaying an astonishing array of taxidermy, these galleries contain sobering statistics on the rate at which species are becoming extinct.

The gallery of **Fish, Amphibians and Reptiles** includes some fascinating species, such as the fish that live between between the sea's twilight zone at 1,300ft (400m) and total darkness at 3,300ft (1,000m). Next door is the serene **Marine Invertebrates department**, where cabinets of corals, shells and sea fans are enhanced by the sound of waves breaking on a shore.

Earth Galleries

Head through Waterhouse Way in the direction of the museum's other main

Natural History Museum   *Dinosaurs, the star attraction*

section: the Earth Galleries. This section is brought to life by exciting special effects and atmospheric sound and lighting. A central escalator transports visitors into a gigantic rotating globe. At the top, the **Restless Surface** section looks at earthquakes and volcanoes. The tremors of an earthquake are simulated in a mock-up of a Japanese mini-market; and a bank of television sets next to a car covered in volcanic ash replays news reports of the 1991 eruption of Mt Pinatubo in the Philippines.

In **From the Beginning**, the story of the universe is told, from the time of the Big Bang 15,000 million years ago to the end of the solar system, which is pencilled in for 5,000 million years from now. Finally, demonstrating the sheer beauty our planet has to offer, is the **Earth's Treasury** gallery, which displays rocks, gems and minerals glittering in semi-darkness.

SCIENCE MUSEUM

Just around the corner on Exhibition Road is the third museum developed after the success of the 1851 Great Exhibition, the **Science Museum** ❸ (www.sciencemuseum.org.uk; daily 10am–6pm; free). This museum traces the history of inventions from the first steam train to the space rocket and has more than 10,000 exhibits, plus additional attractions such as an Imax cinema.

Ground floor
The museum's ground floor is home to **Exploring Space** and **Making the Modern World**. The former's highlight is a replica of the *Apollo 11* lunar excursion module, but look out also for the videos of early rocket experiments in the 1920s.

Making the Modern World (with 'modern' defined as post-1750) brings together many of the museum's prize exhibits. Here you can find the world's oldest surviving steam locomotive, *Puffing Billy* (*c*.1815), Stephenson's pioneering *Rocket* passenger locomotive (1829) and the battered *Apollo 10* command module (1969).

Third floor
Head up to the third floor for the magnificent **Flight Gallery**, with exhibits ranging from a seaplane to a Spitfire to hot-air balloons. Here too is the 1919 Vickers Vimy, in which Alcock & Brown made the first non-stop transatlantic flight, and a Messerschmitt rocket-propelled fighter, as well as the first British jet aircraft, the Gloster Whittle E28/39. Visitors can peer into the cockpit of a Douglas DC3 and participate in interactive exhibits illustrating the principles of flight. A flight simulator offers a rodeo-style ride (charge).

Past and future
Now go back downstairs to the basement. As well as a child-oriented area, it houses the **Secret Life of the Home**,

Harrods illuminated at night

a collection of domestic appliances and gadgets that provoke nostalgia in adults and disbelief in children. A range of models charts the development of the electric toaster since 1923. Other everyday items include a 1925 Sol hairdryer and a 1945 Goblin Teasmade.

Other exhibits geared more towards adults include **Energy: Fuelling the Future**, **Health Matters**, **Glimpses of Medical History** and **Psychology: Mind Your Head**, while the games of **In Future** raise intriguing questions for everyone. The Imax Cinema shows stunning science-related films from deep sea adventures, space-related themes and wildlife spectaculars.

KNIGHTSBRIDGE

End the route by walking east along Cromwell Road, which then turns into the Brompton Road. Note, on your left, **Brompton Oratory** ❹ (Thurloe Place; www.bromptonoratory.com; daily 6.30am–8pm; free), a flamboyant Italian Baroque church designed by 29-year-old architect Herbert Gribble.

Department stores

Now head up Brompton Road towards Knightsbridge station. At Nos 87–135, is the famous department store, **Harrods** ❺ (Mon–Sat 10am–8pm, Sun 11.30am–6pm). East End grocer Henry Charles Harrod opened a store here in 1849, in anticipation of trade sparked by the Great Exhibition. The Harrod family sold the company in 1889, but the store still flourished. Construction of the current building, by C.W. Stephens, architect of Claridge's hotel, started in 1901. The Fayed brothers bought the store in 1983, and sold it to the Qatari royal family in 2010.

Highlights include the magnificent Art Nouveau food hall, a good place to buy provisions for a picnic in nearby Hyde Park (see route 12), just north of Knightsbridge. Alternatively, if you want to carry on shopping, continue east on Knightsbridge to the up-market **Harvey Nichols** ❻ department store, or walk south down Sloane Street, which is lined with designer names and leads to the King's Road and Chelsea.

Pastel-coloured mews houses

CHELSEA

A summer afternoon in Chelsea might include a visit to London's oldest garden or the home of a famous writer, followed by a walk along the Thames or one of the capital's most famous shopping streets.

DISTANCE: 3.75 miles (6km)
TIME: Half to a full day
START/END: Sloane Square

Riverside Chelsea was little more than a fishing village until around the 15th century, when it became fashionable with aristocrats who built smart country houses along the King's Road, which was then the private royal route linking Westminster with the palace of Hampton Court to the west.

In the 19th and 20th centuries the area drew artists enticed by the riverside setting and quality of the light. The 1960s marked the peak of its fame, but in the 1980s the area still had some edge, reflected by the opening of Vivienne Westwood and Malcolm McLaren's cult shop, Sex, at 430 King's Road.

Although Westwood's shop, renamed World's End (the name of the part of Chelsea west of the kink in the King's Road) is still there, the area is now far from cutting-edge; instead, it is one of the smartest, and most expensive, parts of London.

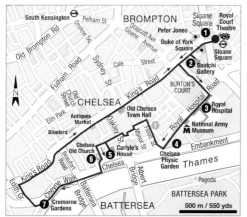

SLOANE SQUARE

Start by the tube, on the eastern side of **Sloane Square ❶**, laid out in

Strolling down King's Road

the late 18th century and named after Sir Hans Sloane, a wealthy physician and collector who purchased the manor of Chelsea in 1712. To your right is the **Royal Court Theatre** (www.royal courttheatre.com), dating from 1870 and with a reputation for staging high-quality new material. The café here is also very good.

Walk along the south side of the square now, and note to your right the department store, **Peter Jones**.

DUKE OF YORK SQUARE

Continue west on the King's Road. On your left is Duke of York Square, a pedestrian enclave of up-market homeware and fashion units, cafés and, in winter, an ice rink. Partridges the grocers organises a regular Saturday food market outside their shop, with lots of enticing things to eat. Behind is the Duke of York's Headquarters, formerly a military campus, but now the home of the **Saatchi Gallery** ❷ (www.saatchi-gallery.co.uk; daily 10am–6pm; free), showcasing contemporary art collected by former advertising mogul Charles Saatchi. He was an early purchaser of work by YBAs (Young British Artists) such as Damien Hirst and Tracey Emin.

ROYAL HOSPITAL

Back on the King's Road with its many fashion and shoe stores, take the next left, Cheltenham Terrace. At the end, continue on to Franklin's Row, which joins Royal Hospital Road.

In front of you is the **Royal Hospital Chelsea** ❸ (www.chelsea-pensioners. org.uk; Mon–Sat 10am–noon and 2–4pm; free), a grand building inspired by the Hôtel des Invalides in Paris and built by Christopher Wren in 1692. This is home to approximately 400 Chelsea Pensioners, retired war veterans who are identifiable by their red uniform coats. Next to the hospital is the **National Army Museum** (www.nam. ac.uk; daily 10am–5.30pm; free).

CHELSEA PHYSIC GARDEN

Continue west along Royal Hospital Road until you reach No. 66 and the **Chelsea Physic Garden** ❹ (www. chelseaphysicgarden.co.uk; Apr–Oct Tue–Fri, Sun 11am–6pm; charge); the entrance is on the left, on Swan Walk. Founded by the Society of Apothecaries in 1676, it is second only to the one in Oxford as the oldest botanic garden in the country. It has thousands of rare and unusual plants, and themed trails for children and adults.

CARLYLE'S HOUSE

At the end of Royal Hospital Road you come to Flood Street, where Margaret and Denis Thatcher once lived at No. 19. Head to the right for the excellent **Coopers Arms**, see ❶. From the pub, go west

Carlyle's House   *Chelsea Physic Garden*

through the area's network of pretty streets – along Alpha Place, over Chelsea Manor Street on to Oakley Gardens, then west on Phene Street and Upper Cheyne Row – to Cheyne Row itself.

Here, at No. 24, time seems to stand still in **Carlyle's House ❺** (www.nationaltrust.org.uk; mid-Mar–Oct Wed–Sun 11am–5pm; charge). The Scottish historian Thomas Carlyle brought his wife Jane to live in this elegant Queen Anne house in 1834.

Their home was turned into a museum in 1896 and remains a time capsule of Victorian life, with papered-over panelling and books, furniture and pictures just as the Carlyles left them.

CHEYNE WALK

At the north end of Cheyne Row turn left into Upper Cheyne Row and Lawrence Street, home of the Chelsea porcelain works from 1745–84. Dr Johnson fancied his hand at the wheel, but his pots never survived the firing. Continue on to Cheyne Walk, one of London's most exclusive streets. Past residents include George Eliot, J.M.W. Turner, Dante Gabriel Rossetti and, more recently, Mick Jagger.

Here, you will be confronted by a lumpen, gilded statue of Sir Thomas More, another famous resident. Henry VIII's chancellor went to the Tower, and was beheaded in 1535, having prepared his resting place in **Chelsea Old Church ❻**. The building was nearly destroyed by a landmine in 1941 but was reassembled from the shattered fragments. Look out for the two carved capitals by Holbein.

Cremorne Gardens

The riverside walk here is attractive, with the sun on the water and houseboats moored by Battersea Bridge, but the road turns away from the river at **Cremorne Gardens ❼**. In Victorian times, party-goers used to dance the night away beneath the coloured lanterns.

BACK TO SLOANE SQUARE

Edith Grove on the right will take you back to the King's Road. A brisk 25-minute walk past its shops (excluding stops) will take you to Sloane Square; alternatively, catch bus Nos 11 or 22 heading east. As you make your way back, look out, on your left, for Terence Conran's renovated Bluebird Garage, at No. 350 and, on the right, halfway along the King's Road, the Old Chelsea Town Hall, a popular spot for celebrity marriages. Flanking the town hall are two antiques markets.

Food and Drink

❶ COOPERS ARMS

87 Flood Street; tel: 020-7376 3120; www.coopersarms.co.uk; daily L and D; ££

Pub serving big portions of British classics.

Parliament Hill

HAMPSTEAD

Full of pretty houses on leafy groves and set against the backdrop of its glorious heath, Hampstead seems the quintessence of an English village. In reality, it is not so much rural idyll as exclusive suburb, a haven in a hectic city.

> **DISTANCE:** 2.75 miles (4.5km)
> **TIME:** Half a day
> **START/END:** Hampstead tube
> **POINTS TO NOTE:** Walk this route Wed–Sun, when the museums open.

Until not so long ago, Hampstead was the home of artists and writers, with such famous residents as John Constable and George Orwell. Its pretty alleys, leafy streets and heath still make this villagey suburb a desirable address.

From **Hampstead tube station**, take Heath Street south (past **The Horseshoe**, see ①) and turn right at Church Row, a street of Georgian houses. Follow the sign to John Constable's grave in the bosky graveyard of **St John's Church ①**, halfway down.

FENTON HOUSE

Head north up Holly Walk, past the one-time home of Scottish writer Robert Louis Stevenson, and turn left to Hampstead Grove. On your left is **Fenton**

House ❷ (Windmill Hill; www.national trust.org.uk; Mar–Oct Wed–Sun 11am–5pm; charge), a grand William-and-Mary mansion built for a merchant. Behind gilded gates, the walled garden, with apple orchard and rose beds, has hardly changed for 300 years. Inside are fine paintings, furniture, porcelain and a collection of harpsichords.

BURGH HOUSE

Back on Hampstead Grove, turn right and descend the steps to Heath Street, then cross over to New End. At the far end of the street is New End Square and **Burgh House ❸** (www.burghhouse. uk; Wed–Fri and Sun noon–5pm; free). Built in 1704, it contains the local his-

Food and Drink

① THE HORSESHOE
28 Heath Street; tel: 020-7431 7206; daily L and D; ££
Good real ales and classic British food.

Keats House interior

tory museum, with a display on painter John Constable.

WILLOW ROAD AND KEATS HOUSE

Continue on to Willow Road. At the far end, overlooking the heath, is the Modernist **2 Willow Road ❹** (www. nationaltrust.org.uk; Mar–Oct Wed–Sun 11am–5pm; charge), designed by architect Ernö Goldfinger for himself. Inside is his art collection, with works by Henry Moore, Bridget Riley, Max Ernst and Marcel Duchamp.

Next, turn right on Downshire Hill, then left on to Keats Grove to **Keats House ❺** (www.cityoflondon.gov.uk; Mar–Oct Tue–Sun 1–5pm, Nov–Mar Fri–Sun only; charge), the Regency villa where the poet lodged before departing for Rome, where he died a year later, in 1821, aged 25. Under a plum tree in the garden he penned one of his best-loved poems, *Ode to a Nightingale*. Inside are his keepsakes of Fanny Brawne, the neighbour with whom he fell in love.

HAMPSTEAD HEATH

At the end of Keats Grove, turn left on to South End Road and take one of the paths on the right on to the heath. Bear north up the hill to **Kenwood House ❻** (www.english-heritage.org.uk; daily Nov–Mar 10am–5pm, Apr–Oct check website; free). This mansion was bequeathed to the nation by brewing magnate, Edward Guinness, and houses his art collection, with works by Rembrandt, Vermeer, Reynolds and Turner. Outside again, stroll across the heath to return to Hampstead tube station.

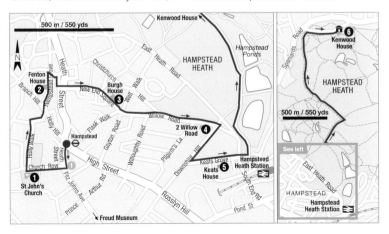

Shopping at Portobello Market

NOTTING HILL

Notting Hill's appeal derives from its fusion of cultures and lifestyles – bourgeois splendour combines with bohemian chic. The best time to come is on a Saturday when Portobello Road market is in full swing.

DISTANCE: 2 miles (3km)
TIME: Half a day
START: Notting Hill Gate tube
END: Westbourne Park tube
POINTS TO NOTE: The Saturday market on Portobello Road gets extremely crowded by mid-morning, so arrive very early to snap up the bargains. There are also some stalls on Fridays and Sundays.

Notting Hill became fashionable in the 1990s, when monied people from the worlds of fashion and media moved in, attracted by the lingering street cred of the mix of ethnic cultures and shabby chic look. The neighbourhood is now extremely expensive.

In the 1800s, however, the area's grand crescents sat next to noxious slums, and as recently as the 1950s, the district was very poor. Large numbers of Afro-Caribbean immigrants settled in overcrowded lodging houses, and the area saw race riots in 1958.

Now different cultures rub along more happily, though the local population has become largely white middle class, and the famous Notting Hill Carnival has become the world's second largest, after Rio.

PORTOBELLO ROAD

Leaving **Notting Hill Gate tube station**, turn right (north) off Notting Hill Gate on to Pembridge Road. Walk past the retro shops and turn left into Portobello Road. The top part of the road is largely residential, with pretty terraces painted different colours. Look for the blue plaque at No. 22, where the writer George Orwell used to live.

Food and Drink

① LISBOA PÂTISSERIE

57 Golborne Road, W10; tel: 020-8968 5242; daily 8am–7.30pm; £

Stop for a coffee and a *pastel de nata* (custard tart) in this popular Portuguese café.

Street market

Further down, beyond the turning for **Westbourne Grove** , you enter the thick of the market for antiques and collectables. Dozens of stalls are hidden away in arcades such as the Admiral Vernon, on your left. Many are open only on Saturdays. Bargaining is expected.

At the **Elgin Crescent** turning, the theme changes to food, with traditional green grocery sitting side by side with organic olive bread. Behind stalls of pak choi and ciabatta, on your left at No. 191, is the **Electric Cinema** (www. electriccinema.co.uk), which screens current films in a vintage setting, with leather armchairs, footrests and wine coolers.

Further up, turn left down **Blenheim Crescent** for **Books for Cooks** (www. booksforcooks.com; Tue–Sat 10am–6pm) at No. 4, a delightful little shop that is, of course, devoted to cookery books, but also offers cookery workshops and has a small café where you can sample the results.

Beyond the Westway

Back on Portobello Road, walk under the concrete **Westway flyover**, where the market becomes a showcase for boho fashion. Boutiques in Portobello Green Arcade sell pink heart-shaped sunglasses and fake fur gilets, while stalls outside sell vintage clothes, old LPs and retro design.

Towards Golborne Road

Continue to the junction with **Golborne Road**, where you should turn right. Here, Moroccan shops sell slippers and spices, and the Portuguese community queues for coffee at the **Lisboa**, see. At the end of the road looms **Trellick Tower**, designed by Ernö Goldfinger. Turn right on Elkstone Road for the tube station.

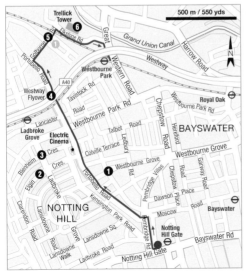

Eclectic items for sale at Spitalfields Market

THE EAST END

Where once were slums, race riots and Jack the Ripper are now art galleries, trendy bars and urban cool, while in Canary Wharf, once the docks of Britain's imperial trade, is the power-architecture of investment banks.

DISTANCE: 2.5 miles (4km)
TIME: A full day
START: Whitechapel Art Gallery
END: Geffrye Museum
POINTS TO NOTE: To attend the markets in full swing at Spitalfields or Columbia Road, walk this route on a Sunday.

Long associated with poverty, overcrowding and inner-city grime, the increasingly gentrified East End came under the spotlight as the location of the 2012 Olympic Games, held in Stratford. As well as being home to its indigenous cockneys, the area has historically also been the first stopping-point for immigrants in London and hosts a wide range of ethnicities. Its cultural mix, edgy atmosphere and once-cheap accommodation have also made it popular with artists in the last few decades.

Meanwhile, over in the Docklands, it is the investment bankers who have moved in, housed in skyscrapers and posh riverside apartments on the former docks, once so vital to Britain's imperial trade.

WHITECHAPEL

From Aldgate East tube station, follow the signs to the exit next to the **Whitechapel Art Gallery** ❶ (www.whitechapel.org; Tue–Sun 11am–6pm, Thu until 9pm; free). The gallery was founded in 1897 by a vicar and his wife, who aimed to combat spiritual and economic poverty in the East End, and the building was designed by the Arts and Crafts architect Charles Harrison Townsend. Today, it mounts high-quality exhibitions of contemporary art. There is also an excellent café on the mezzanine level.

Leaving the gallery, turn right along Whitechapel Road to continue the route, or, if you are ready for lunch, turn left towards the **East London Mosque**, where Fieldgate Street, on your right, has some of London's best Pakistani restaurants, including **Tayyabs**, see ❶.

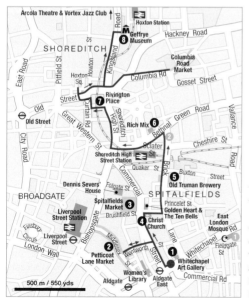

Jumper stall at Spitalfields   *Spitalfields Market*

SPITALFIELDS

London's old markets

Just west of the Whitechapel Gallery, turn into Commercial Street on your right. Heading north, off to your left down Wentworth Street is **Petticoat Lane Market** ❷ (Mon–Fri 10am–4pm and greatly expanded on Sun 9am–3pm), a centre of the rag trade for 400 years.

Further up Commercial Street, on your left, is **Spitalfields Market** ❸, formerly London's wholesale fruit and vegetable market (since 1682), and now hosting stalls selling fashions, jewellery, homewares, second-hand books and with organic food stalls on Sundays.

Eating and drinking

On the other side of the road is **The Golden Heart** pub, renowned for its popularity among the BritArt crowd; the indulgent and eccentric landlady, Sandra Esquilant, was once voted the 80th most important person in the contemporary art world. The ghost of the Quaker prison reformer Elizabeth Fry is supposed to turn off beer taps in the cellar from time to time. A little further along, on the corner of Fournier Street, is **The Ten Bells** pub, where Jack the Ripper eyed up his victims before murdering them.

Christ Church Spitalfields

On the other corner of Fournier Street is **Christ Church** ❹ (www.cc spitalfields.org; Mon–Fri 11am–4pm, Sun 1–4pm; free), one of Nicholas Hawksmoor's finest works. It was built from 1714–29 to underline the power of the Church of England to the dissenting Huguenots who had settled in the area after fleeing Catholic France. Walking down Fournier Street you pass

Geffrye Museum

the fine houses the Huguenots built once they had grown wealthy from silk weaving and silver smithing.

Brick Lane – 'The Curry Mile'

At the end of the street, turn left on to Brick Lane, famous for its cheap curry houses, thanks to another immigrant community, this time the Bangladeshis.

Crossing Brick Lane is Princelet Street, with some fine early 18th-century houses intact. Further up is the **Old Truman Brewery** ❺, which houses shops, studios, bars, restaurants, nightclubs

---

The Docklands

From c.1700, London's docks grew as the hub of Britain's imperial trade, but in the 1960s their demise came quickly, as trade moved to the deepwater ports required for the new container shipping. By 1980, all London's docks were closed, leaving behind derelict land, unemployment and poverty. The 1990s brought regeneration, with the building of the capital's second major financial district, the Canary Wharf complex. Its main tower, at 800ft (244m), was Britain's tallest building until the Shard was built (see route 10). Take a ride on the Docklands Light Railway (DLR) from Bank to Greenwich to get an idea of the mix of old and new, rich and poor, then visit the Museum in Docklands at West India Quay or Mudchute City Farm on Pier Street.

---

and, on Sundays, a craft market. Towards the end of the street, among the boutiques and cafés of this now-fashionable area, is a much-loved relic of its once sizeable Jewish community – **Beigel Bake**, see ❶, on your left.

HOXTON AND SHOREDITCH

At the top of Brick Lane, turn left on to Bethnal Green Road. On your right is **Rich Mix** ❻ (www.richmix.org.uk; Mon–Fri 9am–11pm, Sat–Sun 10am–11pm), a former garment factory, which now houses a cinema, art galleries and recording studios. Just beyond is the crossroads with Shoreditch High Street, where you turn right.

This area was very heavily bombed during World War II, and suffered severe depopulation thereafter – by 1960, St Leonard's Church on the High Street had no parishioners left. Regeneration only took root in the 1990s, when artists moved in, attracted by the cheap studio space. With their success, galleries, bars and nightclubs followed – and higher prices.

Rivington Place

Located on your left, just off the High Street, is Rivington Street. On the right is London's newest public gallery, **Rivington Place** ❼ (www.rivingtonplace. org; Tue–Fri 11am–6pm, Thu until 9pm, Sat noon–6pm; charge). Devoted to cultural diversity, the building hosts art exhibitions and film screenings. Its

Columbia Road flower market

latticed facade was inspired by a Sowei tribal mask.

Hoxton Square

At the end of Rivington Street, turn right on to Curtain Road and left on to Old Street. The first turning on your right is for Hoxton Square. It was here that playwright Ben Jonson killed Gabriel Spencer in a duel in 1598. Today it is a focus of the contemporary art scene in the East End and a fashionable night-life spot.

A detour off the square to the left, past **Sh!**, a boudoir-style women-only sex shop, brings you to Pitfield Street. At No. 17 is **Bookartbookshop**, selling limited-edition artists' books, while at No. 45 is a relic of tatty old Hoxton: **Charlie Wright's International Bar** (www.charliewrights.com; daily until the small hours), where the eponymous former weight-lifter presides over his dive of a bar, where you can listen to jazz or dance to 1980s tracks.

Geffrye Museum

Returning to Old Street, head east, and at the crossroads turn left on to Kingsland Road. (On Sundays go straight on for the Flower Market on **Columbia Road**, the first right off Hackney Road.) Further up Kingsland Road, on your right is the **Geffrye Museum ❸** (www.geffrye-museum.org.uk; Tue–Sun 10am–5pm; free). Housed in former almshouses, built in 1714, this interior-decoration museum first opened in

1914 as a resource and inspiration for workers in the East End furniture trade. It is set up as a series of period rooms taking you from 1600 to the present day. There is also a series of 'period gardens' outside.

In the area are many Vietnamese restaurants. For evening entertainment, take a bus further up Kingsland Road for, on your left, the **Vortex Jazz Club** (11 Gillett Square; www.vortexjazz.co.uk) and, tucked away on Ashwin Street off to the right, near Dalston Lane, the fringe-style **Arcola Theatre** (www.arcolatheatre.com).

Food and Drink

① TAYYABS

83 Fieldgate Street; tel: 020-7247 9543; www.tayyabs.co.uk; daily L and D; £
Chaotic, often long queues, but good food (and prices). Delicious Seekh kebabs – succulent and tasty. Bring your own alcohol (no corkage).

② BEIGEL BAKE

159 Brick Lane; tel: 020-7729 0616; 24 hours daily; £
Perfect plump, soft beigels. Fillings of smoked salmon, cream cheese, herring, or, best of all, salt beef carved off the joint in front of you. Good with mustard and gherkins. Also onion platzels, chollah bread, and stupendous cakes. All very cheap. Cheerful staff.

Passing Monument station

ROUTEMASTER BUS TRIP

Take your furled brolly and Bowler hat and hop on the no. 15 from the Tower of London to Trafalgar Square, via St Paul's Cathedral. 'All aboard for Ludgate Circus!' shouts the conductor. Ding ding. And the bus trundles off…

DISTANCE: 2.75 miles (4.5 km)
TIME: 25 minutes
START: Tower Hill
END: Trafalgar Square
POINTS TO NOTE: The no. 15 bus ride takes 25 minutes but can take longer in rush hour, running daily every 15 minutes 9.30am–6.30pm in both directions. Not every no. 15 is a Routemaster, so wait until one arrives. Conductors accept Travelcards, Oystercards or cash fares.

Turn right as you leave Tower Hill station, towards the Tower of London. Cross the road via the subway and ascend the steps to your left for the bus stop.

EASTCHEAP AND OLD BAILEY

Once on the bus, on your right is the grand **Port of London Authority building ❶**. Then on your left, just past the Tower of London is **All Hallows Church ❷**, the City's oldest, dating from 675. Next, driving up Great Tower Street, on

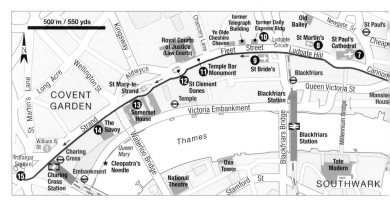

Routemaster on the Strand

your right, up Mincing Lane, you glimpse **The Gherkin ❸**, Norman Foster's peculiarly shaped office tower.

As the street becomes Eastcheap, on the right is Sir Christopher Wren's **Church of St Margaret Pattens ❹**. Soon after, on the left is **Pudding Lane**, where the Great Fire of 1666 began; it is commemorated by the column of **The Monument ❺**. The bus crosses King William Street, which leads left to **London Bridge**, and right towards the Bank of England and, in the distance, the **Barbican Tower**.

Now on Cannon Street, to your right is Wren's **St Stephen Walbrook ❻** and rising up behind, the 1970s' **Tower 42**, once Britain's tallest skyscraper. Next on the right is **St Paul's Cathedral ❼**, while to the left is the Millennium Bridge to **Tate Modern**. Moving on to Ludgate Hill, on the right, is **St Martin's Church ❽**, and beyond, the **Old Bailey**, the scene of many famous criminal trials.

FLEET STREET AND STRAND

Past Ludgate Circus on to Fleet Street, you will see **St Bride's Church ❾**, which inspired the tiered wedding cake, on the left, down Bride Lane. On the right are the black Art Deco former newspaper offices of the **Daily Express ❿** and, shortly afterwards, at no. 135, those of **The Telegraph**. Next on the right is **Ye Olde Cheshire Cheese**, one of the City's oldest pubs, followed by the **Law Courts** towards the end of Fleet Street.

The start of the Strand is marked by the dragon of the **Temple Bar monument ⓫**, set in the middle of the road, and soon afterwards, Wren's **St Clement Danes ⓬**, the church of the Royal Air Force. Then, to the left of the other island church, **St Mary-le-Strand**, is **Somerset House ⓭**, now a major art museum. Shortly afterwards on the same side of the road is the **Savoy Hotel ⓮**.

Finally, the bus rolls into **Trafalgar Square ⓯**. You'll be in need of refreshment, so repair to the **Café in the Crypt**, see ❶.

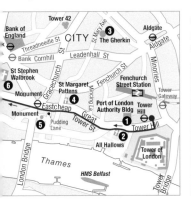

Food and Drink

❶ CAFÉ IN THE CRYPT

Basement, St Martin-in-the-Fields, Trafalgar Square; tel: 020-7766 1158; Mon–Wed 8am–8pm, Thur–Sat till 9pm, Sun 11am–6pm; ££

An atmospheric spot under a church.

Greenwich Park and Canary Wharf

GREENWICH

Compared to central London, Greenwich has a stately but sedate feel. With buildings by Sir Christopher Wren and Inigo Jones, the royal park and a majestic river frontage, it evokes the full splendour of British maritime history.

DISTANCE: 2 miles (3km)
TIME: A full day
START: Cutty Sark
END: Greenwich Park
POINTS TO NOTE: To reach Greenwich, take a boat from Westminster or Tower of London pier (www.thamesriverservices.co.uk), or the Docklands Light Railway (DLR) to Cutty Sark station, or a mainline train from London Bridge.

Of the various ways to get to Greenwich, you could take a boat, just as Queen Elizabeth I used to do, in her state barge rowed from Whitehall to her palace here. The boat today drops you off by the *Cutty Sark* clipper, the starting point for this tour. The dlr also deposits you near the quayside. If you take the train, the *Cutty Sark* is five minutes' walk away – turn left on to Greenwich High Road and follow the road round as it veers left at St Alfege Church. The *Cutty Sark* soon comes into view, ahead to your right.

ALONG THE RIVER

The Cutty Sark

The **Cutty Sark** ❶ (www.rmg.co.uk/cuttysark; daily 10am–5pm) was a clipper that transported tea from China and, later, wool from Australia. Launched in Scotland in 1869, she was the last and fastest of these ships and finally retired in 1922. The ship's name comes from Robert Burns' poem, *Tam O'Shanter*, in which Tam meets a group of witches, all of whom are ugly, but for one, who is young and beautiful and wears only a 'cutty sark' – a short chemise or shirt; the ship's figurehead represents this witch. Unfortunately, while undergoing restoration in 2007, the ship was badly damaged by fire but reopened in April 2012.

Greenwich Foot Tunnel

Also on the river front is the round pavilion containing the entrance to the **Greenwich Foot Tunnel** ❷ (daily 24 hours; free). The tunnel was completed in 1902 and allowed south London residents to walk to work at the docks on

Old Royal Naval College gate
Old Royal Naval College gate

The Cutty Sark

the Isle of Dogs on the north side of the river. Inside, a lift and a long spiral staircase take you down 50ft (15m) to the tunnel, lined with 200,000 glazed white tiles.

River path

Now walk east along the river path past the two blocks of the **Royal Naval College**. The gap between them ensured that the Queen's House (to your right) had unobstructed views of the river. For similarly excellent views of the Thames, you could refuel at the **Trafalgar Tavern**, see ❶.

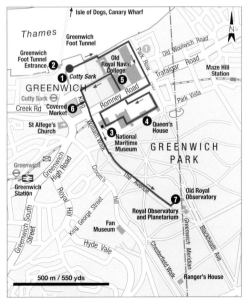

MARITIME MUSEUM

From Park Row, take a right turn at Romney Road and cross over to the **National Maritime Museum** ❸ (www.1.rmg.co.uk; daily 10am–5pm; free). The museum is formed from the Queen's House and two wings, joined by colonnades.

The public collection is housed in the larger west wing, with permanent displays on naval history, polar exploration, colonialism and oceanography. Highlights include the Royal Barge of 1732, decorated with lions, dragons and monsters; and the Nelson gallery (with the tunic he was wearing when fatally wounded at Trafalgar – you can even see the musket-ball hole). Short, free talks and tours are run throughout the day.

The west wing also now benefits from a large extension, the Sammy Ofer Wing, which houses a permanent gallery Voyagers: Britons and the Sea, a café, a rooftop restaurant, library and a shop.

The Queen's House

Now walk along the colonnade to the **Queen's House** ❹ (times as for the National Maritime Museum). Construction

The ceiling of the Painted Hall

on this, England's first Palladian villa, began in 1616, to designs by Inigo Jones. Intended for James I's Queen Anne, it was only completed after her death, and was then given by Charles I to Henrietta Maria. She stayed here only briefly, as the Civil War broke out in 1642.

Today, the house is used to display the National Maritime Museum's art collection, with seascapes and portraits by, among others, Joshua Reynolds and Thomas Gainsborough. The real attraction, however, is the architecture, which is sublime and deceptively simple: the Tulip Stairs, for example, were the first centrally unsupported spiral stairs constructed in England.

The Ranger's House

On the western edge of Greenwich Park, on Chesterfield Walk, is the Ranger's House (www.english-heritage.org.uk; Apr–Sept Sat–Wed 11.30am–4pm, guided tours only; charge). An elegant Georgian villa built in 1723, it became the official residence of the 'Ranger of Greenwich Park' after 1815, when the post was held by Princess Sophia Matilda, niece of George III. Today it houses the art collection of diamond magnate Sir Julius Wernher (1850–1912). Among the 700 items are early religious paintings, Dutch Old Masters, carved Gothic ivories, Renaissance bronzes and fine silver.

NAVAL COLLEGE

Now cross over the road again and enter the **Old Royal Naval College** ❺ (www.ornc.org; daily grounds 8am–6pm, hall and chapel 10am–5pm; free) by the Romney Road Gate. Built on the site of the Tudor royal palace of Placentia (birthplace of Elizabeth I), the complex was founded in 1694 as a hospital for elderly and infirm seamen. Sir Christopher Wren was appointed architect, and laid out all the foundations early on, so that future architects would have to fulfil his master plan.

By the 19th century, British naval supremacy meant fewer casualties of war, and during the 1860s the hospital closed. In 1873 the Royal Naval College moved in; young officers were trained here until 1998, when the College passed to the Greenwich Foundation.

Today, only the 'Painted Hall' and the chapel are open to the public. The Painted Hall was originally intended as the dining room for the hospital. Unfortunately, Sir James Thornhill took so long to paint it (1707–26) and made it so elaborate (he was paid by the yard) that injured sailors never got to eat there, and it became a tourist attraction. In 1806, Admiral Lord Nelson's body lay in state here following his death at the Battle of Trafalgar; over three days, up to 30,000 people came to view the body.

The chapel, completed in 1789, is an unaltered example of the Greek-revival style of James 'Athenian' Stuart, with its

Skaters in Greenwich Park

classical columns and motifs. Worthy of contemplation inside is the altarpiece by the American painter, Benjamin West; it depicts the story of St Paul's shipwreck on the island of Malta.

COVERED MARKET

Leave the Naval College grounds by the west side on to King William Walk and cross the road to the **Covered Market** ❻ (www.greenwich-market.co.uk; Tue–Sun 10am–5.30pm). Here, you can browse the stalls selling food, jewellery, clothing, toiletries and gifts, as well as the shops alongside.

GREENWICH PARK

From the Covered Market, return to King William Walk and head south, down the side of the Maritime Museum and through the gates into **Greenwich Park** (www.royalparks.org.uk; daily 6am–dusk; free).

Observatory and Planetarium
Follow the park's main road up the hill to the **Old Royal Observatory** ❼ (www.rmg.co.uk/royalobservatory; daily 10am–5pm; free). Founded by Charles II in 1675 for the study of astronomy and the fixing of longitude, it was designed by Wren (an amateur astronomer) for Flamsteed, the Astronomer Royal, who lived and worked here until his death in 1719. Today, scientific instruments on display include sundials, atomic clocks, and Harrison's marine chronometers.

On the roof is a time ball, erected in 1833. At 12.55pm every day the ball rises up the pole, reaching the top at 12.58pm, and then dropping at exactly 1pm. The ball can be seen clearly from the river, and ships used to use it to check their time. In the courtyard below, brass strips set in the ground mark the **Greenwich Meridian**, the line dividing the eastern and western hemispheres.

Nearby is the South Building, housing the **Planetarium** (school term times Mon–Fri 12.45–4.15pm, Sat–Sun and school holidays 11am–5pm; shows every 45 minutes; charge).

After admiring the view, wander back to the town, though if you have children you may want to visit the boating pond and playground near the east wing of the Maritime Museum.

Food and Drink

❶ TRAFALGAR TAVERN
6 Park Row; tel: 020-8858 2909;
www.trafalgartavern.co.uk; Mon–Sat L and
D, Sun L until 4pm; ££
Historic pub built in 1837, where Victorian politicians celebrated the end of the parliamentary session with fish dinners. It was also popular with Thackeray, Wilkie Collins and Dickens, who set the wedding breakfast scene in *Our Mutual Friend* here. Bar food plus more formal meals at the Collingwood Restaurant.

The Palm House

KEW

This southwest London suburb is synonymous with the 300-acre (120-hectare) royal botanic gardens, which contain more than 30,000 types of plants, dozens of follies, glasshouses, lakes, ponds and even a Chinese pagoda. This route shows you some of its highlights and allows a leisurely ramble around the rest.

DISTANCE: 2 miles (3km)
TIME: Half to a full day
START/END: Kew Gardens tube
POINTS TO NOTE: Kew is on the Richmond branch of the District line. Alternatively, take an overland train from Waterloo to Kew Bridge.

In the leafy suburb of Kew are the **Royal Botanic Gardens** (www.kew.org.uk; Apr–Oct Mon–Fri 9.30am–6pm, Sat–Sun until 7.30pm, Nov–Mar 9.30am–4.15pm; glasshouses and museums close half an hour earlier than gardens; charge, children free). Passing into royal hands in the 1720s, the gardens were created by Prince Frederick, son of George II, in 1731. His widow, Augusta, introduced the botanical element in 1759, and the grounds were subsequently landscaped by that most renowned of all gardeners, 'Capability' Brown. Kew became famous, though, when the botanist Sir Joseph Banks returned in 1771 from his global travels with Captain Cook, bringing back many strange and exotic plants, and cultivating them in the royal gardens here.

PALM HOUSE AND LAKE

Enter the gardens by the **Victoria Gate** ❶, then pick up a map and head north towards the **Palm House** ❷, which fronts on to a lake. Designed by Decimus Burton, the Palm House was completed in 1848 and was the first large-scale wrought-iron structure of its kind. Each of its iridescent panes of glass is hand-blown. Inside, climb up the spiral stairs through the steamy tropical atmosphere to the galleries and

---

Food and Drink

❶ THE ORANGERY

Kew Gardens; tel: 020-8332 5686; www.kew.org; daily B, L and AT, 10am until an half hour before gardens close; ££
Never successful as a hothouse for oranges, this classical building is a fine setting for a restaurant.

Tree in Kew Gardens   *Kew Palace*

inspect the canopy of banana trees, coconuts and pawpaws.

In the basement is the **Marine Display**, with tanks of corals, fish, algae and mangrove swamps. Just to the side of the Palm House is the **Waterlily House ❸**, encompassing a circular pond covered in giant Amazonian water lilies.

Outside, on the opposite side of the lake, another Decimus Burton creation, Museum No. 1, houses the **Plants and People Exhibition ❹**, which illustrates mankind's dependence on plants, with exhibits displayed in the museum's fine original Victorian mahogany cabinets.

PRINCESS OF WALES CONSERVATORY

Continuing northeast beyond the lake, follow the signs for the **Princess of Wales Conservatory ❺**. This glasshouse is divided into 10 microclimates, suitable for everything from cacti to carnivorous plants. It is particularly worth seeking out the *titan arum* – equally renowned for being the world's largest flower, for its foul smell (like rotting flesh) and for its rare flowerings.

KEW PALACE

Next, heading northwest, take some refreshment at the **Orangery**, see ❶, en route to **Kew Palace ❻** (Apr–Oct daily 9.30am–5.30pm; charge). Originally built for a Dutch merchant, Britain's smallest palace was leased to Queen Caroline in 1728 for 'the rent of £100 and a fat Doe'. George III later bought the palace and recuperated here during his first period of madness. The garden behind is laid out in 17th-century style with parterres of box and herbs, ornamented with statuary.

DIRECTORY

Hand-picked hotels and restaurants to suit all budgets and tastes, organised by area, plus select nightlife listings, an alphabetical listing of practical information and an overview of the best books and films to give you a flavour of the city.

The Ritz

ACCOMMODATION

London's hotels are famously expensive, and foreign visitors can be disappointed by the standard provided for the high rates charged. But fortunately, this is less true than it used to be. New hotels offering affordable accommodation in a central location, many belonging to mid-range chains, have sprung up in areas such as the South Bank and the City, and even top-end hotels offer special deals.

London has everything from grand hotels of international renown to family-run hotels, guesthouses, self-catering flats and youth hostels. The choice of accommodation can make or break a visit to the capital, and the flip-side of the massive choice is the equally massive prices often charged.

However, there are bargains to be had. As with most things, you need to shop around. If a clean room and a hot breakfast are all you ask, a small hotel may offer them for about a sixth of the price of a top hotel. The smaller hotels are often more friendly, making up in the welcome what they may lack

in facilities. Just don't expect a lot of space – the cheaper rooms really are cell-like. If you are a light sleeper, bear in mind that central London is quite noisy, both by day and night. Enquire about noise levels and remember that in small hotels, rooms at the rear are often quieter.

Most hotels have free wi-fi in the lobby areas.

Hotel areas

There are hotels everywhere in London, but some areas have more than others. Don't necessarily expect to find a bargain two minutes' walk from Piccadilly Circus, though the main concentrations tend to be around Victoria, Earl's Court/Kensington, the West End and Bayswater. SW1 is London's traditional hotel district. There are some delightfully old-fashioned hotels in Victoria, in most price brackets, and the streets close to Victoria Station are full of terraced bed-and-breakfast accommodation. There are also streets full of terraced (or rather town houses, for this is Kensington) hotels in the second big hotel area of SW5 and SW7. This zone, around Kensington High Street, Earl's Court and Gloucester Road, is another major centre for medium-range hotels of dependable comfort.

The West End is the third area and the best-known zone. You'll pay more

> Price for a double room for one night without breakfast:
> ££££ = over £300
> £££ = £200–300
> ££ = £120–200
> £ = below £120

Pool at One Aldwych   *One Aldwych bedroom*

for budget or moderate accommodation here than you will in SW1 or SW5. W1 hotels at the bottom end of the price range can be very humble. WC1 is a clever choice: it's central and has reasonable prices, and there is still some dignity, even romance, in Bloomsbury (don't expect to find either quality in Oxford Street).

Bayswater, or at least the area between Edgware Road, Bayswater Road, Paddington and Queensway, is full of hotels. It does have a few large expensive hotels on its fringes but has a greater concentration of moderate and budget accommodation. Quality and prices vary enormously but the area is convenient for the West End.

Budget Chains

Premier Inn is Britain's biggest budget hotel chain, with several outposts in central London, including County Hall (by Westminster Bridge), Euston, Kensington, Southwark and Tower Bridge. There are also branches close to Gatwick and Heathrow. They are clean, modern and cost between £80 and £100 per night. Central reservations: 0871 527 9222, www.premier inn.com.

The expanding **Travelodge** chain does a similar job at similar prices; book early for good deals: www.travelodge.co.uk. Other reputable chains include **Best Western** (tel: 08457 767 676; www.bestwestern.co.uk), **Holiday Inn** (tel: 0871 423 4896; www.holidayinn.com)

and **Thistle** (tel: 0871 376 9099; www.thistle.com) which often have hotels in prime locations.

Covent Garden and Soho

Covent Garden Hotel
10 Monmouth Street, WC2; tel: 020-7806 1000; www.firmdale.com; tube: Covent Garden; £££

Understatedly chic boutique hotel. As well as 58 rooms styled with a contemporary English aesthetic, the hotel also offers a luxurious film screening room, a DVD library, a gym and beauty salon.

Hazlitt's
6 Frith Street, W1; tel: 020-7434 1771; www.hazlittshotel.com; tube: Tottenham Court Road; ££

In the heart of Soho, this gorgeous converted 1718 house has impressive literary connections. Rooms are in period style, and modern luxuries subtly tucked away.

One Aldwych
1 Aldwych, WC2; tel: 020-7300 1000; www.onealdwych.co.uk; tube: Temple, Covent Garden; ££££

Trying a little too hard, with corporate artworks and a pool with underwater music, this hotel nevertheless offers good service in a great location.

St Martin's Lane
45 St Martin's Lane, WC2; tel: 020-7300 5500; www.stmartinslane.com; tube: Leicester Square; ££££

This Starck/Schrager collaboration is one of the most stylish hotels in town. Rooms have high windows and mood-lighting options. Well placed for West End theatres.

Sanderson Hotel

50 Berners Street, W1; tel: 020-7300 1400; www.sandersonlondon.com; tube: Oxford Circus; ££££

Another Starck/Schrager creation, and the acme of their modernism-meets-theatre ethos. The Long Bar and Suka restaurant are destinations in themselves, and the spa is fittingly opulent.

The Savoy

Strand, WC2; tel: 020-7836 4343; www.fairmont.com/savoy; tube: Charing Cross; ££££

One of London's great institutions, with a reputation for comfort and personal service, reopened after a dramatic £100-million revamp. Conveniently situated for theatreland and Covent Garden.

Soho Hotel

4 Richmond Mews, W1; tel: 020-7559 3000; www.firmdalehotels.com; tube: Tottenham Court Road; £££

With bold, modern design touches in Kit Kemp's signature style, this hotel feels luxuriously urban, with dramatic drawing rooms and a buzzing bar.

W Hotel

Leicester Square, 10 Wardour Street, W1; tel: 020-7758 1000; www.wlondon.co.uk; tube: Leicester Square; ££££

The extraordinary design of the building and its prominent position have already made this new hotel a London landmark. The ultra-sleek nightclub feel of the interior has also made it a fashionable place to be seen.

Mayfair and Piccadilly

Brown's Hotel

30 Albemarle Street, W1; tel: 020-7493 6020; www.brownshotel.com; tube: Green Park; ££££

Opened in 1837 by Lord Byron's butler, James Brown, this classic luxury hotel is now owned by Rocco Forte. The interior has been redesigned with a contemporary, elegant look.

Claridge's

Brook Street, W1, tel: 020-7629 8860; www.claridges.co.uk; tube: Bond Street; ££££

For many, the embodiment of English hotel graciousness. The rooms are elegant late Victorian or Art Deco in style, and top chef Gordon Ramsay runs the restaurant.

The Connaught

16 Carlos Place, W1; tel: 020-7499 7070; www.the-connaught.co.uk; tube: Bond Street; ££££

One of the best hotels in London, and very popular with British visitors. Discreet but immaculate service, and a restaurant with one Michelin star. Only 90 rooms.

W Hotel

Cumberland Hotel

Great Cumberland Place, W1; tel: 0871 376 9014; www.guoman.com; tube: Marble Arch; ££

Sleek minimalist decor both in the public rooms and the hi-tech guest rooms. Celebrity chef Gary Rhodes runs the restaurant. Good business facilities.

The Dorchester

Park Lane, W1; tel: 020-7629 8888; www.dorchester.com; tube: Hyde Park Corner; ££££

Large luxury hotel. The rooms have traditional decor and some have views over Hyde Park. The spa and the prestige restaurants – including China Tang and the three-Michelin-starred Alain Ducasse – are the main draw for many.

Duke's Hotel

35 St James's Place, SW1; tel: 020-7491 4840; www.dukeshotel.com; tube: Green Park; £££

Traditional hotel with gas-lamps lighting the courtyard, and an intimate atmosphere. The comfortable rooms are decorated in a classic, understated style. Quality without ostentation.

Durrants Hotel

George Street, W1; tel: 020-7935 8131; www.durrantshotel.co.uk; tube: Marble Arch; ££

A traditional family-run hotel in a Georgian terrace. Rooms are comfortable, with some antique furnishings.

The Four Seasons

Hamilton Place, Park Lane, W1; tel: 020-7499 0888; www.fourseasons.com/London; tube: Hyde Park Corner; ££££

This is a temple of modern opulence overlooking Hyde Park. Friendly and efficient service. Luxury spa.

The Lanesborough

1 Lanesborough Place, SW1; tel: 020-7259 5599; www.lanesborough.com; tube: Hyde Park Corner; ££££

Deluxe hotel overlooking Hyde Park Corner. The stately neoclassical facade of the former St George's hospital complements the opulent Regency-style interior. Despite being a relative newcomer this is one of London's finest hotels.

Lincoln House Hotel

33 Gloucester Place, W1; tel: 020-7486 7630; www.lincoln-house-hotel.co.uk; tube: Marble Arch; £

Georgian-style bed-and-breakfast hotel, with well-equipped rooms.

Metropolitan by Como

19 Old Park Lane, W1; tel: 020-7447 1000; www.comohotels.com; tube: Green Park; ££££

Synonymous with late-1990s celebrity hedonism, the bar is the most noted feature of this modern hotel. The rooms, however, are also worthy of mention, graced as they are with clean simple decor and abundant natural light.

Metropolitan by Como room

Montcalm Hotel

34–40 Great Cumberland Place, W1;
tel: 020-7958 3200; www.montcalm.co.uk;
tube: Marble Arch; ££

Quiet, comfortable mid-range hotel in an elegant Georgian crescent. Features low-allergen bedrooms.

No. 5 Maddox Street

5 Maddox Street, W1; tel: 020-7647 0200;
www.living-rooms.co.uk; tube: Bond Street;
£££

Suites-cum-flats with minimalist, Eastern-inspired decor and full facilities including well-stocked kitchens.

Park Plaza Sherlock Holmes

108 Baker Street, W1; tel: 020-7486 6161;
www.parkplazasherlockholmes.com; tube:
Baker Street; ££

Ignore the connotations of the name: this is a boutique hotel with modern guest rooms, a gym and a steam room.

Pavilion

34–6 Sussex Gardens, W2; tel: 020-7262
0905; www.pavilionhoteluk.com; tube:
Edgware Road; £

Eccentric hotel where each room has a different theme, from 'Casablanca Nights' to 'Enter the Dragon'.

The Ritz

150 Piccadilly, W1; tel: 020-7493 8181;
www.theritzlondon.com; tube: Green Park;
££££

The gilded lustre has long since faded, and this now slightly shabby hotel relies on its famous name to draw people in for highly priced afternoon teas. Men must wear jackets and ties in public rooms; no jeans or trainers allowed.

Westminster and Victoria

41

41 Buckingham Palace Rd, SW1; tel:
020-7300 0041; www.41hotel.com; tube:
Victoria; ££££

You can't sleep closer to Buckingham Palace than in this posh 30-room boutique hotel with full amenities and club-like atmosphere.

Airways Hotel

29–31 St George's Drive, SW1; tel: 020-
7834 0205; www.airways-hotel.co.uk;
tube: Victoria; £

A pleasant hotel close to Buckingham Place and Westminster Abbey. 40 en-suite rooms.

B&B Belgravia

64–6 Ebury Street, SW1; tel: 020-7259
8570; www.bb-belgravia.com; tube:
Victoria; £

Chic, modern B&B offering good value for the style and facilities. These include: free DVD and internet use, a choice of organic breakfasts, and free bicycle hire.

Blair Victoria Hotel

78–84 Warwick Way, SW1; tel: 020-7828
8603; www.blairvictoria.com; tube: Victoria;
£

Attractive period hotel close to the train and bus stations. 48 rooms.

The Met Bar   *Suite at The Ritz*

Dover Hotel
42–44 Belgrave Rd, SW1; tel: 020-7821 9085; www.dover-hotel.co.uk; tube: Victoria; £
Friendly B&B hotel three minutes' walk from Victoria station. 13 rooms.

Eccleston Square Hotel
37 Eccleston Square, SW1; tel: 0800-3746 8357; www.designhotels.com; tube: Victoria; ££
Behind the facade of a smart stuccoed 19th-century town house is probably the most technologically sophisticated hotel in London. Each room has a huge 3-D television and DVD player, an iPad2, and electronic settings for everything from the bed and the curtains to lighting and temperature.

Georgian House Hotel
35-39 St George's Drive, SW1; tel: 020-7834 1438; www.georgianhousehotel. co.uk; tube: Victoria; ££
Friendly and well-run bed and break-fast hotel close to Victoria station. 53 rooms.

Goring Hotel
15 Beeston Place, Grosvenor Gardens, SW1; tel: 020-7396 9000; www.thegoring. com; tube: Victoria; ££££
This family-owned, delightfully tradi-tional hotel near Buckingham Palace has a relaxed old-world atmosphere.

Sanctuary House Hotel
33 Tothill Street, SW1; tel: 020-7799 4044; www.sanctuaryhousehotel.co.uk; tube: St James's Park; ££
Small, recently refurbished hotel above a Fullers Ale and Pie House.

Kensington and Chelsea

Aster House
3 Sumner Place, South Kensington, SW7; tel: 020-7581 5888; www.asterhouse.com; tube: South Kensington; £££
Victorian townhouse B&B, well located for the famous museums. The rooms have chintzy fabrics, Wi-fi and power showers in the bathrooms.

Beaufort Hotel
33 Beaufort Gardens, SW3; tel: 020-7584 5252; www.thebeaufort.co.uk; tube: Knightsbridge; £££
Soft, neutral colours are indicative of the calm that prevails at this small, designer hotel. Attentive service. Cream teas and residents' bar included in the room rate.

Berkeley Hotel
Wilton Place, SW1; tel: 020-7235 6000; www.the-berkeley.co.uk; tube: Knightsbridge; ££££
Many rate the Berkeley as the best in London. Elegantly low-key, it offers a country-house atmosphere, a fine spa and rooftop pool, and restaurants run by Marcus Wareing and Gordon Ramsay.

Blakes Hotel
33 Roland Gardens, SW7; tel: 020-7370 6701; www.blakeshotel.com; tube: South

Room at The Halkin

Kensington; ££££

Anouska Hempel's original design hotel. The discreet exterior belies the splendid rooms, designed variously in romantic, grand and exotic styles.

Cadogan Hotel

75 Sloane Street, SW1; tel: 020-7235 7141; www.cadogan.com; tube: Sloane Square; ££££

An Edwardian-styled hotel with a whiff of scandal permeating its traditional formality. Edward VII's mistress Lillie Langtry lived at the Cadogan, and Oscar Wilde was arrested here.

Capital Hotel

22-24 Basil Street, SW3; tel: 020-7589 5171; www.capitalhotel.co.uk; tube: Knightsbridge; ££££

This small luxury hotel in the heart of Knightsbridge offers restrained decor, friendly service and a fine restaurant.

Draycott Hotel

26 Cadogan Gdns., SW3; tel: 020-7730 6466; www.draycotthotel.com; tube: Sloane Square; ££££

This is country-house living, minutes away from Sloane Square and the King's Road. The charming Victorian house is set in a smart residential street and many of the luxuriously appointed bedrooms overlook a tranquil communal garden. 35 rooms.

easyHotel

14 Lexham Gardens, W8; tel: 07951-440 134; www.easyhotel.com; tube: Gloucester Road; £

While this is certainly a no-frills experience (some rooms don't even have a window), it is ideal for budget travellers, and has other branches in London. Internet bookings only.

Enterprise Hotel

15–25 Hogarth Rd, SW5; tel: 020-7373 4502; www.enterprisehotel.co.uk; tube: Earl's Court; £

Good location close to Kensington High Street and Earl's Court tube station. 100 small but functional en suite rooms.

Garden Court Hotel

30–31 Kensington Gardens Sq, W2; tel: 020-7229 2553; www.gardencourthotel. co.uk; tube: Bayswater; ££

Friendly, family-run 32-room bed and breakfast set in a traditional English garden square.

The Gore

189 Queen's Gate, SW7; tel: 020-7584 6601; www.gorehotel.com; tube: South Kensington; £££

Idiosyncratic hotel close to the Royal Albert Hall. Every inch of the walls is covered in paintings and prints, and the themed rooms are decorated with antiques and many a theatrical flourish.

The Halkin by Como

5–6 Halkin Street, SW1; tel: 020-7333 1000; www.comohotels.com; tube: Hyde

Capital Hotel bar   *Draycott Hotel*

Park Corner; ££££
This modern five-star hotel, done out in a minimalist Italian aesthetic, is calm and cosseting, if a little impersonal. Houses London's only Michelin-starred Thai restaurant.

Hotel Indigo
34–44 Barkston Gardens, SW5; tel: 020-7373 7851; www.barkstongardens.com; tube: Earl's Court; ££
Set in a quiet tree-lined street in a Victorian terrace, but close to the bustle of Earl's Court and the world-class museums of South Kensington. Meals available. 93 rooms, all with private bath.

The Nadler
25 Courtfield Gardens, SW5; tel: 020-7244 2255; www.thenadler.com; tube: Earl's Court; £
Taking the principles and style of boutique hotels to the budget market, this hotel offers 'studios', with their own fridges, microwaves and media facilities.

The Rockwell
181 Cromwell Road, SW5; tel: 020-7244 2000; www.therockwell.com; tube: Earl's Court; ££
Decorated in a contemporary homely style, the rooms feel cheerful and airy.

Vicarage Private Hotel
10 Vicarage Gate, W8; tel: 020-7229 4030; www.londonvicaragehotel.com; tube: Notting Hill Gate; £
Friendly place, with clean, simple rooms and good English breakfasts.

Bloomsbury and Holborn

Academy Hotel
21 Gower Street, WC1; tel: 020-7631 4115; www.theacademy hotel.co.uk; tube: Goodge Street; ££
A welcoming boutique hotel, situated in five interlinked town houses. Comfortable rooms with traditional decor.

Charlotte Street Hotel
15–17 Charlotte Street, W1; tel: 020-7806 2000; www.firmdalehotels.com; tube: Goodge Street; £££
Combines old-fashioned quality and contemporary style, with soft colours and bold touches. There is a luxurious cinema in the basement.

Crescent Hotel
49–50 Cartwright Gardens, WC1; tel: 020-7387 1515; www.crescenthoteloflondon.com; tube: Russell Square, Euston; £
Simple but pleasant family-run hotel in a Georgian building. Also has access to private gardens and tennis courts.

Gower House Hotel
57 Gower St, WC1; tel: 020-7636 4685; www.gowerhousehotel.co.uk; tube: Goodge Street; ££
Pleasant bed-and-breakfast hotel near the British Museum.

Holiday Inn Bloomsbury

Coram St, WC1; tel: 0871-423 4901;
www.holidayinn.com; tube: Russell Square;
£££
Modern, pleasant hotel with small indoor
pool and leisure club. 313 rooms, all with
private bath.

Hotel Russell

Russell Square, WC1; tel: 020-7837 6470;
www.hotelrusselllondon.co.uk; tube: Russell
Square; ££
A Bloomsbury landmark with opulent
public spaces and individually styled
bedrooms in calm understated colours.

Montague on the Gardens

15 Montague St, WC1; tel: 020-7958 7731;
www.montaguehotel.com; tube: Russell
Square; £££
A pretty period property with a garden at
the rear. Flamboyant decor.

The City and East London

ANdAZ

40 Liverpool Street, EC2; tel: 020-7961
1234; www.london.liverpool street.andaz.
hyatt.com; tube: Liverpool Street;
£££
ANdAZ fits designer facilities into a Victorian railway hotel. Rooms are simple
and contemporary in style.

Crowne Plaza London Shoreditch

100 Shoreditch High St, E1; tel: 0871-423
4876; www.ichotelsgroup.com; tube: Old
Street; £££

Situated in the heart of the City, within
striking distance of Spitalfields Market.
Has 264 rooms and a roof-top restaurant. Like many City hotels, weekend
rates are considerably cheaper than
weekday rates.

Fox & Anchor

115 Charterhouse Street, Smithfield, EC1;
tel: 020-7250 1300; www.foxandanchor.
com; tube: Barbican; ££
This immaculately restored pub has
six individually styled rooms combining
modern comforts with period features.

The Hoxton Urban Lodge

81 Great Eastern Street, Old Street, EC2;
tel: 020-7550 1000; www.hoxtonhotels.
com; tube: Old Street; £
The well-designed rooms offer outstanding value and the latest in hipster
chic. Watch the website for the periodic
offers of rooms for only £1.

Malmaison

Charterhouse Square, Clerkenwell, EC1;
tel: 0844-693 0656;
www.malmaison.com; tube: Barbican;
£££
Atmosphere and style without sky-high
rates in a beautiful Victorian building. Rooms are designed with stylish fabrics and smart bathrooms; the
brasserie and bar come highly recommended.

The Rookery

12 Peter's Lane, Cowcross Street; tel: 020-

7336 0931; www.rookeryhotel.com; tube: Farringdon; £££

Has wood panelling, stone-flagged floors, and open fires. Spacious rooms combine the historic with the contemporary: 18th-century beds and flat-screen TVs.

South Place Hotel

3 South Place, EC2; tel: 020-3503 0000; www.southplacehotel.com; tube: Moorgate; £

This sleek boutique hotel is within walking distance of the Museum of London and Barbican Centre and includes a fitness centre and a spa. You can eat alfresco on the Rooftop Terrace.

Threadneedles

5 Threadneedle Street, EC2; tel: 020-7657 8080; www.hotelthreadneedles.co.uk; tube: Bank; £££

Located in a former bank building, this five-star hotel blends modern comforts with Victorian splendour, from the lovely stained glass dome in the lobby to the restaurant's modern British cuisine.

The Zetter

86–8 Clerkenwell Road, EC1; tel: 020-7324 4444; www.thezetter.com; tube: Farringdon; ££

A quirky designer hotel in a converted warehouse. Second-hand books and hot-water bottles are thoughtful extras in the chic, comfortable rooms. Also check www.thezettertownhouse.com in nearby St John Square.

London Bridge Hotel

8–18 London Bridge St, SE1; tel: 020-7855 2200; www.londonbridgehotel.com; tube: London Bridge; £££

Independent four-star hotel in an efficient location for Bankside's attractions. Has 138 rooms, a gym, two restaurants and a bar.

Mad Hatter

3–7 Stamford Street, SE1; tel: 020-7401 9222; www.madhatterhotel.co.uk; tube: London Bridge, Southwark; ££

Large, colourful, contemporary-styled rooms above a Fullers pub, just a short stroll from Tate Modern.

Mercure London Bridge Hotel

75–79 Southwark St, SE1; tel: 020-7660 0683; www.mercure.com; tube: Southwark; ££

A French chain hotel close to Tate Modern and the Globe Theatre.

Novotel City South

53–61 Southwark Bridge Rd, SE1; tel: 020-7660 0676; www.novotel.com; tube: London Bridge; £

Close to Shakespeare's Globe and Tate Modern. Clean, modern rooms.

Southwark Rose

43–47 Southwark Bridge Road, SE1; tel: 020-7015 1480; www.accorhotels.com; tube: London Bridge; ££

Sleek, simply designed hotel with clean, minimalist lines. Friendly staff.

Grilled halibut at The Ivy

RESTAURANTS

Food from all over the world as well as good British staples, and chefs with innovative ways of preparing fresh home-grown ingredients, can be found in a wide range of prices and environments throughout the capital.

Covent Garden and Soho

Andrew Edmunds

46 Lexington Street, W1; tel: 020-7437 5708; daily L and D; tube: Piccadilly Circus; £££

Soft candlelight and wood panelling make this place cosy and intimate. Dishes are simple but varied, ranging from beef to well-presented pasta. The staff are relaxed and friendly.

Hummus Bros

88 Wardour St, W1; tel: 020-7734 1311; www.hbros.co.uk; Mon–Sat L & D, Sun D only daily; tube: Piccadilly Circus; £

Very popular budget café serving, as its name suggests, hummus with various toppings such as salad or Mexican beef. Ideal mopped up with fresh pitta bread.

> Price guide for an average two-course meal for one with a glass of house wine:
> ££££ = over £40
> £££ = £25–£40
> ££ = £15–25
> £ = below £15

The Ivy

1 West Street, WC2; tel: 020-7836 4751; www.the-ivy.co.uk; daily L and D; tube: Covent Garden; £££

A place to see and be seen, and the food is a secondary consideration, though still of excellent quality (British classics plus international favourites). The waiting staff are delightful, too. The downside is the difficulty in getting a table: reserve weeks, not days, ahead.

Koya

49 Frith Street, W1; tel: 020-7434 4463; www.koya.co.uk; daily L and D; tube: Leicester Square; ££

There's always a queue outside, and they don't take reservations. The udon noodles, and pork belly, at this minimalist Japanese canteen are stupendous.

L'Escargot Marco Pierre White

48 Greek St, W1; tel: 020-7439 7474; www.lescargotrestaurant.co.uk; L Mon–Fri, D Mon–Sat; tube: Tottenham Court Road; £££ (set menu ££)

The grand-père of London's French restaurants, with its lovely 1920s decor, is now run by Marco Pierre White. It offers a choice between the exciting hubbub of the ground floor or the more intimate Picasso room upstairs, with à la carte and set menus.

Chinatown fare   *Rules*

Mildreds

45 Lexington Street, W1; tel: 020-7494 1634; www.mildreds.co.uk; Mon–Sat L and D; tube: Piccadilly Circus; £

Sleek and stylish vegetarian restaurant which offers porcini and ale pie and Malaysian coconut curry.

Mr Kong

21 Lisle Street, WC2; tel: 020-7437 7341; www.mrkongrestaurant.com; daily L and D; tube: Leicester Square; ££

One of the more authentic Chinese restaurants in the area. Dishes include Kon Chi baby squid with chilli sauce or sandstorm crab. Vegetarian options.

Rules

35 Maiden Lane, WC2; tel: 020-7836 5314; www.rules.co.uk; daily L and D; tube: Covent Garden; £££

Established in 1798, the decor reflects its heritage and the food has stood the test of time with high-quality British ingredients: beef, lamb and game from Rules' own estate. Booking advisable.

J Sheekey

28–35 St Martin's Court, WC2; tel: 020-7240 2565; www.j-sheekey.co.uk; daily L and D; tube: Leicester Square; £££

A paradise for fish lovers, in a series of panelled rooms hung with black-and-white theatre prints: specialities include chargrilled squid with gorgonzola polenta, Cornish fish stew and New England baby lobster. Pre-theatre dinners a speciality. Reserve.

Mayfair and Piccadilly

Benares

12a Berkeley Square House, Berkeley Square, W1; tel: 020-7629 8886; www.benaresrestaurant.com; daily L and D; tube: Bond Street; £££

Atul Kochhar's Benares is one of the few Indian restaurants in Europe to win a Michelin star. Dishes include Goan-style lobster Masala in coconut and cinnamon sauce. Reservations essential.

Criterion Grill

224 Piccadilly, W1; tel: 020-7930 0488; www.criterionrestaurant.com; Mon–Sat L and D; tube: Piccadilly Circus; £££

This beautifully restored Victorian restaurant has a simple menu of French classics, all decently prepared. The opulent neo-Byzantine interior is wonderful, and the pre-theatre set menu is reasonably priced.

Greens Restaurant and Oyster Bar

36 Duke Street, SW1; tel: 020-7930 4566; www.greens.org.uk; Mon–Sat L and D; tube: Green Park; £££

Clubby St James's stalwart. Traditional dishes include potted shrimps and lemon sole with perfect hollandaise. Excellent cheeseboard.

Guinea Grill

30 Bruton Place, W1; tel: 020-7499 1210; www.theguinea.co.uk; Mon–Fri L and D, Sat D; tube: Oxford Circus, Green Park; £££

Old-world, wood-panelled place in a

Goring Dining Room

cobbled mews. Great steak and kidney pie, grills and oysters. Good choice of beers, wines and ports.

Le Gavroche

43 Upper Brook Street, W1; tel: 020-7408 0881; www.le-gavroche.co.uk; Mon–Fri L and D, Sat D only; tube: Marble Arch; ££££

Chef Michel Roux Jr offers haute cuisine in the grand style, and the three-course set lunch at £52.60, including half a bottle of wine per person, coffee and water, is a bargain. Undoubtedly one of London's best restaurants.

Scotts

20 Mount Street, W1; tel: 020-7495 7309; www.scotts-restaurant.com; daily L and D; tube: Marble Arch, Green Park; £££

This revamped institution continues to serve delicious fish dishes, including rarities such as stargazy pie. The old-fashioned puddings get a modern twist.

Sketch

9 Conduit Street, W1, tel: 020-7659 4500; www.sketch.uk.com; Lecture Room Tue–Sat L and D, Gallery daily D only; tube: Bond Street, Oxford Circus; ££££

It's decadently over-designed, and super-chef Pierre Gagnaire's food is dizzily priced. Choose between the haute cuisine Lecture Room (two Michelin stars) and the more informal Gallery, where, apparently, 'art meets food meets fashion'.

Westminster and Victoria

Bistrot on the Square

37 Eccleston Square, SW1; tel: 020-3489 1000; www.ecclestonsquarehotel.com; daily B, L (advance bookings only), AT and D; tube: Victoria; ££

Stylish restaurant in the Eccleston Square Hotel serving old favourites from kedgeree to steak and chips, and club sandwiches to schnitzels, all executed with care and panache.

Boisdale

15 Eccleston St, SW1; tel: 020-7730 6922; www.boisdale.co.uk; L Mon–Fri, D Mon–Sat; tube: Victoria; ££££

Classic Scottish restaurant serving dishes such as lobster bisque, haggis and Aberdeen Angus steaks. Live jazz every night and a full malt whisky line-up.

Cinnamon Club

30–2 Great Smith Street, SW1; tel: 020-7222 2555; www.cinnamonclub.com; Mon–Fri B, L and D, Sat L and D; tube: St James's Park; ££££

More like a colonial club than the Old Westminster Library it once was. The haute cuisine take on Indian cooking is innovative and tasty, and the wines complement the spicy food well.

Goring Dining Room

Goring Hotel, Beeston Place, SW1; tel: 020-7396 9000; www.thegoring.com; L Sun–Fri, D daily; tube: Victoria; ££££

Alfresco dining

Traditional fare such as potted shrimps, filet of venison, and proper puddings. Sunday roast lunch is a speciality.

La Poule au Pot

231 Ebury Street, SW1; tel: 020-7730 7763; www.pouleaupot.co.uk; daily L and D; tube: Sloane Square; ££
This romantic spot has been here for 30 years. Everything is very fresh and very French. Good-value set lunches.

Le Caprice

Arlington House, Arlington St, SW1; tel: 020-7629 2239; www.le-caprice.co.uk; L & D daily; tube: Green Park; ££££
Chic, buzzy bistro with Art Deco decor. The food – sophisticated salads, seafood and wonderful desserts – is more for picking over than wolfing down. Vegetarian dishes are also available.

Quaglino's

16 Bury St, SW1; tel: 020-7930 6767; www.quaglinos-restaurant.co.uk; L & D Mon–Sat; tube: Green Park; £££
Glamorous brasserie that also does a set lunch menu. Live music most Friday and Saturday nights adds to the atmosphere.

Smith Square Café and Restaurant

St John's, Smith Square, SW1; tel: 020-7222 2779; L Mon–Fri, D on weekday concert evenings and weekends; tube: St James's Park; ££

Beneath one of London's top concert venues, this brick-vaulted restaurant offers good food and excellent service. Sandwiches and snacks are also on offer, and there is a long wine list.

The Vincent Rooms

Westminster Kingsway College, Vincent Square, SW1; tel: 020-7802 8391; www.westking.ac.uk/thevincentrooms; Mon–Fri L and D; tube: St James's Park; ££–£££
Britain's top catering college (where Jamie Oliver trained) serves the day's results to the paying public. Quality ingredients, often superb execution, pleasant surroundings and reasonable prices.

Kensington and Chelsea

Bibendum

Michelin House, 81 Fulham Road, SW3; tel: 020-7581 5817; www.bibendum.co.uk; daily L and D; tube: South Kensington; £££
Located in the Art Deco Michelin building. Chef Matthew Harris maintains high standards. Grilled oysters with curried sauce and courgette linguine are faultless, the wine list is good and service excellent. Good-value fixed-price lunch menus. Reserve.

Bluebird

350 King's Road, SW3; tel: 020-7559 1000; www.bluebird-restaurant.co.uk; L & D daily; tube: South Kensington; ££
The emphasis at this skylit restaurant, café and bar is on seasonal ingredients. It's a popular place for Sunday brunch,

Chef preparing food

especially on sunny days when you can sit out in the courtyard.

Cadogan Arms

298 King's Rd, SW3; tel: 020-7352 6500; www.thecadoganarmschelsea.com; L & D daily; tube: South Kensington; £££
Traditional Victorian pub turned fashionable gastro-pub, offering real ales along with good food. Dishes might include rack of Welsh lamb or pan fried sea bass. Good selection of British cheeses.

Cambio de Tercio

163 Old Brompton Road, SW5; tel: 020-7244 8970; www.cambiodetercio.co.uk; daily L and D; tube: Gloucester Road; £££
This bright, cheery little restaurant has won many accolades for its exciting food and impeccable service. Some think it is the best Spanish restaurant in town.

Cheyne Walk Brasserie

50 Cheyne Walk, SW3; tel: 020-7376 8787; www.cheynewalkbrasserie.com; L Tue–Sun, D daily (last booking 9pm on Sun); tube: South Kensington; £££ (weekday lunch menu ££)
The flavours of Provence are cooked up over the central grill of this Belle Époque dining room. Also offers views of the Albert Bridge and a sumptuous cocktail lounge.

Chutney Mary

535 King's Road, SW10; tel: 020-7351 3113; www.chutneymary.com; Mon–Fri D only, Sat–Sun L and D; tube: Fulham Broadway; £££
First-class Indian restaurant with stylish decor and exceptional food. The chefs come from across the subcontinent, so take your pick of regional dishes.

Eight Over Eight

392 King's Rd, SW3; tel: 020-7349 9934; www.rickerrestaurants.com; L & D daily; tube: South Kensington; £££
This stylish restaurant offers Asian dishes with a modern twist. Dim sum, sushi, king prawn curry, and chocolate pudding with green tea ice cream are just some of the delights on offer.

Elistano

25–27 Elystan St, SW3; tel: 020-7584 5248; www.elistano.com; L & D daily; tube: South Kensington; £££
The menu varies with the seasons, but it might feature *zucchini fritti* (fried courgettes with mint), and *saltimbocca romana*. The pannacotta is delicious.

Itsu

118 Draycott Avenue, SW3; tel: 020-7590 2400; www.itsu.com; Mon–Sat 11am–11pm, Sun noon–10pm; tube: South Kensington; £
Take away or eat-in at this brightly-lit restaurant. If you don't fancy the incredibly fresh sushi or sashimi, try a dish from the hot grill such as chicken teriyaki. Bookings not accepted.

Burgers are all the rage   *Tom's Kitchen*

Poissonnerie de L'Avenue

82 Sloane Avenue, SW3; tel: 020-7589 2457; www.poissonnerie.co.uk; L & D daily; tube: South Kensington; £££ (set menu ££)

Run by the same family for over 40 years, it serves fresh fish and seafood from the adjoining fishmonger's. Dishes are old-school French, although some come with an Italian flourish.

Racine

239 Brompton Road, SW3; tel: 020-7584 4477; www.racine-restaurant.com; daily L and D; tube: South Kensington; £££

Behind the smart glass exterior classic French fare is cooked with panache. The three-course set menu, available till 7.30pm, offers very good value for this part of town.

Restaurant Gordon Ramsay

68–9 Royal Hospital Road, SW3; tel: 020-7352 4441; www.gordonramsay.com; Mon–Fri L and D; tube: Sloane Square; ££££

The decor is minimalist, the experience impeccable. One of only four restaurants in Britain with three Michelin stars. Try chargrilled monkfish tail with crispy duck. Prices are high so consider the excellent set lunch menu.

Tom Aikens

43 Elystan Street, SW3; tel: 020-7584 2003; www.tomaikens.co.uk; Tue–Fri L and D, Sat D only; tube: South Kensington; ££££

Michelin-starred modern French restaurant. Intensely flavoured dishes such as pig's head braised with spices and ginger demonstrate Aikens' culinary craftsmanship and flair.

Tom's Kitchen

27 Cale St, SW3; tel: 020-7349 0202; www.tomskitchen.co.uk; B and L Mon–Fri, brunch Sat–Sun, D daily; tube: South Kensington; £££

Relaxed brasserie run by award-winning chef Tom Aikens. The menu changes daily, but features classic British dishes such as Cumberland sausages and mash, steak sandwiches, fish pie and macaroni cheese.

Bloomsbury and Holborn

Cigala

54 Lamb's Conduit Street, WC1; tel: 020-7405 1717; www.cigala.co.uk; L and D daily; tube: Russell Square; £££

Buzzing Spanish neighbourhood restaurant offering tapas or à la carte dishes under the aegis of owner-chef Jake Hodges (ex-Moro in Clerkenwell). Excellent sherries, wines and liqueurs. Good-value set lunch menus.

Cosmoba

9 Cosmo Place, off Southampton Row, WC1; tel: 020-7837 0904; www.cosmoba. co.uk; L & D Mon–Sat; tube: Russell Square; ££

A hidden gem in an alley connecting Southampton Row and Queen Square. Unpretentious and run by the same

Fryer's Delight

family for 65 years, Cosmoba specialises in homely Italian food, such as
gnocchi with gorgonzola, or grilled sea
bream.

Fryer's Delight

19 Theobald's Road, WC1; tel: 020-7405
4114; Mon–Sat noon–11pm; tube: Holborn;
£

One of the few remaining fish and chip
shops in central London.

North Sea Fish Restaurant

7–8 Leigh St, WC1; tel: 020-7387 5892;
www.northseafishrestaurant.co.uk; L & D
Mon–Sat; tube: Russell Square; £

Veteran chippie serving straightforward
fish and chips, but also a good range of
fish, including Dover sole, plaice, halibut, trout and scampi, plus British puddings. You may see lots of black cabs
parked outside as London cabbies get
a discount here.

Pied à Terre

34 Charlotte Street, W1; tel: 020-7636
1178; www.pied-a-terre.co.uk; Mon–Fri L
and D, Sat D only; tube: Goodge Street;
££££

Fitzrovia's most prestigious restaurant under chef Marcus Eaves has two
Michelin stars. The eight-course tasting
menu is £80, but set lunch is a bargain.

Salaam Namaste

68 Millman St, WC1; tel: 020-7405 4636;
www.salaam-namaste.co.uk; L & D daily;
tube: Russell Square; ££

A light and modern restaurant which
won the award for best chef of the year
in the 2013 Asian Curry Awards. Excellent pan-Indian cuisine with a special
emphasis on seafood. Lots of famil-
iar Indian dishes, but many inventive
options too.

Ye Olde Cheshire Cheese

145 Fleet St, EC4; tel: 020-7353 6170;
Mon–Sat L and D; tube: Chancery Lane; ££

This is easily dismissed as a tourist trap,
but its age and history are impressive:
it was frequented by many famous Londoners, including Dickens and Samuel
Johnson. A warren of nooks and cran-
nies, its cosy chop room serves good
steak and kidney pies.

The City and East London

Browns Restaurant & Bar

Unit A, Hertsmere Rd, E14; 020-7987 9777;
www.browns-restaurant.co.uk; L & D daily;
tube: Canary Wharf; £££

Traditional British atmosphere and classics such as salmon fishcakes. Sunday
roasts are popular, with dishes such as
rib of beef or pork loin served with vegetables and roast potatoes.

Coach & Horses

26–8 Ray Street, EC1; tel: 020-7278 8990;
www.thecoachandhorses.com; Mon–Fri L
and D; tube: Farringdon; ££

One of the best of the gastro-pubs. The
scrubbed-wood decor is simple, the
food inventive but unpretentious, the
wines well priced and the service good.

Fish and chips   *Ye Olde Cheshire Cheese*

Comptoir Gascon

61–3 Charterhouse Street, EC1; tel: 020-7608 0851; www.comptoirgascon.com; Tue–Sat L and D; tube: Farringdon; £££

An informal, tapas/bistro-style version of Club Gascon, on West Smithfield. Southern French dishes are cooked at both places.

The Eagle

159 Farringdon Road, EC1; tel: 020-7837 1353; Mon–Sat L and D, Sun L only; tube: Farringdon; ££

Pub serving reasonable food with a Mediterranean bias, complemented by an extensive range of European beers. Gets crowded quickly, so arrive early.

Eyre Brothers Restaurant

70 Leonard St, EC2; tel: 020-7613 5346; www.eyrebrothers.co.uk; L Mon–Fri, D Mon–Sat; tube: Old Street; ££££

Adventurous fusion of Iberian-influenced meat and vegetable dishes. Simple, distinct flavours. Tapas menu available.

Fifteen

15 Westland Place, N1; tel: 020-3375 1515; www.fifteen.net; daily L and D; tube: Old Street; £££

Run by Jamie Oliver, every year this restaurant apprentices disadvantaged young people into its kitchen and tries to transform them into Italian chefs that even The River Café would be proud of. Even if the dishes are not always perfectly executed, it is fascinating to see this project in action.

Fox & Anchor

115 Charterhouse Street, Smithfield, EC1; tel: 020-7250 1300; www.foxandanchor. com; daily B, L and D; tube: Barbican; ££

Old-fashioned British cooking in a lovingly restored pub. Try the oysters with a pint of stout (in a pewter tankard), followed by ham hock, steak and oyster pie or the daily roast. Prices are very reasonable and the atmosphere relaxed. Highly recommended.

Les Trois Garçons

1 Club Row, E1; tel: 020-7613 1924; www.lestroisgarcons.com; Thu–Fri L, D Mon–Sat; tube: Old Street; ££££ (set dinner £££)

Extravagantly decorated (stuffed tigers, etc) ex-pub with French food. The nearby Loungelover cocktail bar run by the same people is the perfect place for a pre- or post-dinner drink.

Moro

34–6 Exmouth Market, EC1; tel: 020-7833 8336; www.moro.co.uk; Mon–Sat L and D, Sun D only; tube: Farringdon; ££

The excellent food on Moro's lively Spanish–North African menu includes charcoal grilled lamb and wood-roasted pork. Friendly service.

The Real Greek & Mezedopolio

6 Horner Square, Old Spitalfields Market, E1; tel: 020-7375 1364; www.therealgreek. com; daily L and D; tube: Shoreditch High Street; ££

Mezze regulars are moussakas, tiny shellfish and tomato cutlets. Main

courses include lamb or beef pasta dishes, and there are distinctive cheeses and pastries.

Royal China

30 West Ferry Circus, E14; tel: 020-7719 0888; www.royalchinagroup.co.uk; L & D daily; tube: Canary Wharf; £££

Upmarket Chinese restaurant with a beautiful terrace overlooking the Thames. Serves up great Chinese specialities and fabulous dim sum (until 4.30pm only).

St John

26 St John Street, EC1; tel: 020-7251 0848; www.stjohngroup.uk.com; Mon–Fri L and D, Sat D only, Sun L only; tube: Farringdon; £££

A stone's throw from Smithfield meat market, this restaurant is stark but elegant. The meat- and offal-heavy menu changes with the season. Chef Fergus Henderson's signature roast bone-marrow and parsley salad is always on the menu, and whole roast suckling pig may make an appearance.

Smiths of Smithfield

66–7 Charterhouse Street, EC1; tel: 020-7251 7950; www.smithsofsmithfield.co.uk; daily B, L and D; tube: Farringdon; £££ (brunch Sat–Sun ££)

Brunch on a Saturday or Sunday is great fun in this buzzing post-industrial complex. Tuck into a cooked breakfast, grilled minute steak, or corned beef hash. The restaurant upstairs is more refined and more expensive.

Sông Quê

134 Kingsland Road, E2; tel: 020-7613 3222; L and D daily; tube: Old Street; £

Vietnamese restaurant with a huge menu (28 types of noodle soup). Fresh, aromatic food. Friendly service.

The South Bank

The Anchor and Hope

36 The Cut, SE1; tel: 020-7928 9898; Tue–Sat L and D, Sun L only, Mon D only; tube: Waterloo; ££

All the produce here is British, and the meat – featured strongly on the menu – is butchered on the premises. Try the perfectly cooked roast neck of lamb with ratatouille. Keen prices, hefty portions and friendly staff. No reservations.

Butlers Wharf Chop House

Butlers Wharf Building, 36e Shad Thames, SE1; tel: 0207-7403 3403; www.chophouse-restaurant.co.uk; L & D daily; tube: Tower Hill; ££££ (set menu ££)

Carnivores should go straight for the steak and kidney pudding, served with oysters, or pork loin and crackling. There are fish dishes for non-meat eaters. Other attractions include great river views and a terrace.

fish!

Cathedral St, SE1; tel: 020-7407 3803; www.fishkitchen.com; B, L & D daily; tube: London Bridge; £££

The River Café

Specialises in tasty GM-free fish in the shadow of Southwark Cathedral. Bar seats are fun but noisy.

Masters Super Fish

191 Waterloo Road, SE1; tel: 020-7928 6924; Tue–Sat L and D; tube: Waterloo; £
Need a taxi? You will find cabbies galore tucking into huge portions of fish and chips in this old-fashioned eatery.

Mesón Don Felipe

53 The Cut, SE1; tel: 020-7928 3237; www.mesondonfelipe.com; Mon–Sat L and D; tube: Southwark; ££
A busy little place with a great atmosphere and lots of tasty tapas. The drinks list is an education in Spanish wines. Bookings taken before 8pm; after that it is first come first served.

Oxo Tower

Oxo Tower Wharf, Barge House St, SE1; tel: 020-7803 3888; www.harveynichols. com; L & D daily; tube: Southwark; ££££ (set lunch £££)
Some find it overpriced, but this iconic spot is still hugely popular. The biggest draw is the fabulous view of the Thames through huge windows.

Le Pont de la Tour

Butlers Wharf Building, 36d Shad Thames, SE1; tel: 020-7403 8403; www.lepontdelatour.co.uk; L & D daily; tube: Tower Hill; ££££ (set lunch £££)
Prime ministers and presidents have enjoyed the splendid view of Tower Bridge from here, where the stress is on seafood. Impeccable but very expensive.

RSJ

33a Coin St, SE1; tel: 020-7928 4554; www.rsj.uk.com; L Mon–Fri, D Mon–Sat; tube: Waterloo; £££
This pretty restaurant offers pleasant dishes such as Gressingham duck with beetroot salad, but the real attraction is the excellent selection of wines from the Loire.

West London

The Galicia

323 Portobello Road, W10; tel: 020-8969 3539; daily L and D; tube: Ladbroke Grove; ££
Chaotic tapas bar and restaurant serving the local Spanish community. Tasty, unpretentious, authentic dishes, such as good rich stews, and some very tempting puddings.

The River Café

Thames Wharf, Rainville Road, W6; tel: 020-7386 4200; www.rivercafe.co.uk; Mon–Sat L and D, Sun L only; tube: Hammersmith; £££–££££
A west London institution, and its reputation for fine Italian food is well deserved (as is its reputation for very high prices). Only the best produce is selected by owner/chef, Ruth Rogers. Dishes such as char-grilled scallops with deep-fried artichokes, beef with tomatoes and spinach are faultless. Booking well ahead is essential.

NIGHTLIFE

These entertainment venues represent a selection of the landmarks of London's vibrant cultural scene. You could also consult www.viewlondon.co.uk or the weekly listings magazine, *Time Out*, which is handed out free on Tuesdays.

Theatre

Holland Park Open Air Theatre
Holland Park, W8; tel: 020-7361 3570; www.operahollandpark.com
During the warm summer months opera, dance and theatre performances are staged here in the semi-open air.

National Theatre
South Bank; tel: 020-7452 3000/3400; www.nationaltheatre.org.uk
One of Britain's most famous modernist buildings contains three theatres, which present a range of modern and classical drama.

The Old Vic
The Cut, near Waterloo Station; tel: 0844-871 7628; www.oldvictheatre.com
This former music hall is now a repertory theatre with a strong reputation. Kevin Spacey is the artistic director.

Open Air Theatre, Regent's Park
Regent's Park; tel: 0844-826 4242; http://openairtheatre.com
With a 16-week summer season, this not-for-profit charity hosts a variety of plays, including Shakespeare.

Royal Court Theatre
Sloane Square; tel: 020-7565 5000; www.royalcourttheatre.com
This stylish venue stages plays by contemporary playwrights. The bar-restaurant in the foyer is ideal for pre-theatre dinners.

Shakespeare's Globe
21 New Globe Walk, Bankside; tel: 020-7902 1400; www.shakespearesglobe.org
A reconstruction of Shakespeare's original open-to-the-elements theatre, the Globe hosts summer seasons of his, and other, plays.

Music

Barbican Arts Centre
Silk Street; tel: 020-7638 8891; www.barbican.org.uk
A purpose-built arts complex with a theatre, cinema, and art gallery as well an impressive concert hall. The venue for the London Symphony Orchestra.

Jazz Café
5 Parkway, Camden NW1; tel: 0844-847 2514 (tickets) or 020-7688 8899 (for a table); www.mamacolive.com
Intimate jazz club in Camden Town that attracts some top names. Tube: Camden.

London Coliseum

London Coliseum

St Martin's Lane; tel: 020-7836 0111;
www.eno.org
This extravagantly decorated Edwardian theatre is home to the English National Opera.

Ronnie Scott's

47 Frith Street; tel: 020-7439 0747;
www.ronniescotts.co.uk
The eclectic musical tastes of Ronnie Scott, who died in 1996, are still reflected in this legendary Soho venue, which has hosted some of the biggest names in jazz since 1959.

Royal Albert Hall

Kensington Gore; tel: 020-7589 8212;
www.royalalberthall.com
This vast rotunda hosts large-scale concerts by ageing rock stars and occasional operatic performances, as well as the Promenade festival of classical concerts throughout the summer.

Royal Festival Hall

Belvedere Road; tel: 020-7960 4200;
www.southbankcentre.co.uk
As well as being the premier classical music venue, this complex offers free Friday lunch time jazz and folk performances in the foyer.

Royal Opera House

Bow Street, Covent Garden; tel: 020-7304 4000; www.roh.org.uk
Home to the Royal Ballet and the Royal Opera, this magnificent theatre has a worldwide reputation.

St John's, Smith Square

Westminster, SW1; tel: 020-7222 2168;
www.sjss.org.uk
This church has been converted into a concert hall hosting chamber music and lunchtime concerts.

St Martin-in-the-Fields

Trafalgar Square, WC2; tel: 020-7766 1100;
www.smitf.org
Concerts (classical and jazz) are held at lunchtimes and evenings in this church.

St Mary-le-Bow

Cheapside, EC2; tel: 020-7248 5139;
www.stmarylebow.co.uk
Lunchtime recitals most Thursdays. Home to the famous Bow bells.

Wigmore Hall,

36 Wigmore Street, W1; tel: 020-7935 2141; www.wigmore-hall.org.uk
Delightful intimate hall with seating for 550. It has a pleasant atmosphere and excellent acoustics and is most renowned for chamber recitals. Also hosts Sunday morning coffee concerts.

Dance

Peacock Theatre

Portugal Street; tel: 020-7863 8198;
www.sadlerswells.com
This outpost of Sadler's Wells in the West End is housed in an uninspiring concrete block, but visitors shouldn't be

put off – the modern dance productions staged here are usually first rate.

Sadler's Wells

Rosebery Avenue; tel: 020-7863 8198; www.sadlerswells.com
This hi-tech theatre near Islington in North London is Britain's top contemporary dance venue.

BFI Southbank

Belvedere Road, South Bank; tel: 020-7928 3232; www.bfi.org.uk
The headquarters of the British Film Institute presents a varied programme of arthouse and off-beat films on three screens.

Curzon Soho

99 Shaftesbury Avenue; tel: 0330-500 1331; www.curzoncinemas.com
This is the flagship in a chain of five arts cinemas in London. The other branches are in Bloomsbury, Chelsea, Mayfair and Richmond. Each branch screens all the latest arthouse releases.

Prince Charles Cinema

7 Leicester Place; tel: 020 7494 3654; www.princecharlescinema.com
The big multiplexes on nearby Leicester Square charge high prices for blockbuster films but this quirky little cinema round the corner offers a more interesting repertory programme at a more modest price.

Bars and Clubs

Café de Paris

3–4 Coventry Street; tel: 020-7734 7700; www.cafedeparis.com
The Café de Paris is a stylish old dancehall which attracts an older crowd that likes to dress up smartly.

Cargo

83 Rivington Street; tel: 020-7739 3440; www.cargo-london.com
This gritty under-the-arches venue is a staple part of big nights out in Shoreditch. Entertainment includes live music, DJs and dancing till late.

EGG

200 York Way; tel: 020-7871 7111; www.egglondon.net
A venue with three dance floors, EGG attracts big-name DJs.

Electric Ballroom

184 Camden High Street; tel: 020-7485 9006; www.electricballroom.co.uk
This old dancehall attracts a mixed crowd with its retro 1970s, 1980s and 1990s nights. Upstairs there's R&B and hip-hop.

Fabric

77A Charterhouse Street, EC1; tel: 0207-7336 8898; www.fabriclondo.com
Celebrated club that mixes big names (generally on Fridays), with top DJs (Saturdays) and new talent. Big on techno and electronica. Open until 6am (8am on Saturdays). Dress code: casual.

Gig at Koko

Gordon's Wine Bar
47 Villiers Street, WC2; tel: 020-7930 1408;
www.gordonswinebar.com
A family-run bar close to Embankment tube, just behind Charing Cross. Quaff fine wines and eat delicious pies and cheeses in the candlelit cellar of a building once inhabited by Samuel Pepys, and, much later, Rudyard Kipling. Seating outside in summer.

Heaven
The Arches, Villiers Street, WC2; tel: 020-7930 2020; www.heaven-live.co.uk
Submerged beneath the Charing Cross development is this famous gay club, home to the legendary G-A-Y club nights. Very casual dress code.

Koko
1A Camden High Street, NW1; tel: 0870-432 5527; www.koko.uk.com.
Venue for club nights and gigs by some of the biggest names in rock and pop.

Ministry of Sound
103 Gaunt Street, SE1; tel: 020-7740 8682; www.ministryofsound.com
This renowned dance club is London's top house-music venue. Open until 7am Sat.

Plan B
418 Brixton Road, SW9: tel: 020-7733 0926; www.planb-london.com
Atmospheric Brixton venue with open warehouse-style interior. Talented house DJs and a buzzing crowd. Dress code: smart and sexy.

Plastic People
147–149 Curtain Road, EC2; tel: 020-7739 6471; www.plasticpeople.co.uk
Deep, heavy sound system in a small but electric venue. Plays mainly dubstep but also hosts DJs who sway towards a more techno sound.

Roxx, Blagclub
68 Notting Hill Gate, W11; tel: 07762 104 373; www.roxxclub.com
Trendy rock and roll club with modern house remixes and live entertainment. Great cocktails and good after-party vibe.

Salsa
96 Charing Cross Road, WC2; tel: 020-7379 3277; www.bar-salsa.com
A good Latin venue in the heart of the West End. Lots of fun, very busy and a good place to practise your moves with regular dance classes. Casual.

Vinoteca
7 St John Street, EC1; tel: 020-7253 8786; www.vinoteca.co.uk
Wines by the glass from a 200-strong list (also retailed from the shop), together with tasty modern European food. Recommended.

333
333 Old Street, EC1; tel: 020-7739 5949; www.333mother.com.
Hip club with a good drinking lounge upstairs and pounding dance music in the basement.

A–Z

A

Airports and arrival

Airports

London has two major international airports: Heathrow, 15 miles (24km) to the west (mainly scheduled flights) and Gatwick, 25 miles (40km) to the south (scheduled and charter flights), plus three smaller airports, Stansted and Luton (north) and London City (east).

Heathrow: The fastest connection to central London is the Heathrow Express (tel: 0845-600 1515; www.heathrow express.com) to Paddington, every 15 minutes, 5.10am–11.45pm, taking 15 minutes. Paddington connects with several tube lines (see map inside back cover). The fare is £20 single. A cheaper option is the 25-minute Heathrow Connect service, which stops at several stations; a single costs £9.50 (tel: 0845-678 6975; www.heathrow connect.com).

There is a direct tube route (www. tfl.gov.uk; £5.50 single) on the Piccadilly line, daily 5am (6am on Sun) until 11.45pm, 55 minutes to central London.

National Express (tel: 0871-781 8178, www.nationalexpress.com) runs coaches from Heathrow to Victoria; journey time 45–80 minutes, depending on traffic; single from £6.

Gatwick: The Gatwick Express (www. gatwickexpress.com) leaves Gatwick for Victoria every 15 minutes, 4.30am– 12.50am. It takes 30 minutes and costs £19.50 one way. Also non-express services to Victoria, London Bridge and King's Cross. Singles from £14.40; 35– 45 minutes.

Stansted: The Stansted Express rail link (www.stanstedexpress.com) goes to Liverpool Street every 15 minutes; journey time 45 minutes; a single costs £23.50.

London City: The DLR stop for London City is six minutes from Canning Town tube (Jubilee line); every 10 minutes from 5.30am–12.50am.

Luton: Luton Airport Parkway is linked by Thameslink services to King's Cross and Blackfriars, every 15 minutes, weekdays only; 45 minutes.

Airport Numbers

Heathrow: tel: 0844-335 1801.
Gatwick: tel: 0844-892 0322.
Stansted: tel: 0844-335 1803.
London City: tel: 020-7646 0088.
Luton: tel: 01582-405 100.

Airport Cabins: If you need to bed down at the airport prior to an early morning flight, consider Yotel (tel: 020-7100 1100; www.yotel.com) at Heathrow's Terminal 4 or Gatwick's South Terminal. Here, check into a luxurious cabin (as if in first class on an aircraft) for a few hours' kip at any time of day

St Pancras station interior

or night. Depending on demand, a double cabin costs about £85 a night, and a single about £60. Prices come down if you stay for less time (minimum 4 hours, from £32). Cabins have en suite bathrooms, a TV-film system and free internet access.

Arrival by train

Eurostar services from Paris Gare du Nord take around 2.25 hours; from Brussels 2 hours, to London St Pancras. For UK bookings, tel: 0870-518 6186; www.eurostar.com.

Vehicles are carried by **Le Shuttle** (tel: 08705-353 535; www.eurotunnel.com) through the tunnel between Folkestone in Kent and Sangatte in France. Two–five departures each hour, and the trip takes 35 minutes. Bookings not essential, but advisable at peak times. Fares vary according to time of travel: late at night or early morning are usually cheaper. Taking a car (with any number of passengers) through the tunnel costs from about £60 single.

B

Blue plaques

The first blue ceramic plaque was erected in 1867 on the front of 24 Holles Street, W1, by the Royal Society of Arts to commemorate Lord Byron, who was born there. Across London there are now around 800 such plaques, commemorating former famous residents. Each one gives the bald facts about the person concerned. The awarding of a plaque is haphazard – many are put up after descendants propose the suggestion to English Heritage; however, the person being remembered must have been dead for at least 20 years. The range has so far been dominated by politicians and artists.

C

Children

Public transport: Up to four children aged 10 years 11 months or under can travel free on the underground if accompanied by an adult. Eleven to 15-year-olds can get much reduced off-peak travel but need an Oyster photocard; buses are free for under 16s, but 11–15year-olds need an Oyster photocard, see www.tfl.gov.uk/tickets for details.

Supplies: Infant formula and nappies (diapers) can be found in chemists (pharmacies) and supermarkets. If you require over-the-counter medications such as Calpol (liquid paracetamol) late at night, Bliss Pharmacy (5 Marble Arch; tel: 020-7723 6116) is open daily until midnight.

Eating out: This need not be an ordeal. Although the maître d's face in many a smart restaurant may fall as you approach with a gaggle of tots in tow, there are some establishments that enjoy catering for children. Try Sticky Fingers (Phillimore Gardens, W8 7QG; www.stickyfingers.co.uk), the children's

Downing Street gates

restaurants in Harrods and Hamley's, or any of the cafés in London's parks. Look out also for branches of Giraffe (Southbank Centre, Spitalfields Market, Brunswick Centre etc), Pizza Express and Carluccio's (all over London), which are usually very child-friendly.

Clothing

London is a great city to explore on foot, so comfortable walking shoes are essential. Bring warm clothes if you're visiting in winter, as the weather can be very chilly, and remember to have something waterproof (or at least an umbrella) with you in spring or autumn, as showers are quite common.

Crime

Hold on to purses, do not put wallets in back pockets, and do not place handbags on the ground in busy restaurants. Gangs of professional thieves target the tube. Use only licensed minicabs and black cabs.

In an emergency, dial 999 from any phone (free). Otherwise telephone the nearest police station, listed under 'Police' in the telephone directory.

Customs regulations

There are no official restrictions on the movement of goods within the European Union (EU), provided those goods were purchased within the EU. However, British Customs (www.hmrc.gov.uk) have set the following personal-use 'guide levels': 3,200 cigarettes or 400 cigarillos or 200 cigars or 3kg tobacco (200 cigarettes or 250g of smoking tobacco if coming from eastern European countries); 10 litres spirits, 20 litres fortified wines, 90 litres wine, 110 litres beer.

Those entering from a non-EU state are subject to these limits: 200 cigarettes or 100 cigarillos or 50 cigars or 250g of tobacco; 2 litres still table wine plus 1 litre spirits (over 22 percent by volume) or 2 litres fortified or sparkling wine or other liqueurs; 60 ml of perfume plus 250 ml of toilet water; £390 worth of gifts, souvenirs or other goods.

There are no restrictions on the amount of currency you can bring in.

Cycling

Route maps for cyclists are available from the London Cycling Campaign (www.lcc.org.uk) or London Cycle Network (www.londoncyclenetwork.org.uk). A bike lending scheme exists whereby you borrow a bike from one of dozens of docking stations all over central London, then leave it at any other docking station. No need to sign up first: just pay the access fee and usage charge at the docking station with a credit or debit card. See www.tfl.gov.uk for a map of locations.

D

Disabled access

An excellent guidebook is *Access in London* by Gordon Couch, William For-

Hiring a Barclays bike

Sign indicating the congestion charge

rester and Justin Irwin (Quiller Press). The London Tourist Board also provides free maps and leaflets, available from Information Centres. For details on public transport see www.dft. gov.uk/transportforyou/access/.

Artsline is a freephone information service for disabled people, covering the arts and entertainment (tel: 020-7388 2227; www.artsline.org.uk).

Driving

Unless you are planning on making several trips outside the capital, a car may be more of a hindrance than a help, thanks to busy traffic and often aggressive drivers, and certainly a considerable expense, owing to the congestion charge (see below) and high parking costs.

If you do hire (or bring) a car, remember to drive on the left and observe speed limits (police detection cameras are common). It is strictly illegal to drink and drive, and penalties are severe. Drivers and passengers must wear seat belts. For further information consult the *Highway Code* (www.gov.uk/browse/driving/highway-code).

Congestion charge: In central London, drivers must pay a congestion charge. The boundaries of the congestion zone, which extends from Kensington in the west to the City in the east, are clearly indicated with signs and road markings. Cars entering this zone Mon–Fri 7am–6pm are filmed and drivers are fined if a payment of

£10 has not been made by midnight the same day (or £12 the following day). You can pay at many newsagents and by phone or online (tel: 0845-900 1234; www.tfl.gov.uk/roadusers).

Fuel: Petrol (gasoline) is sold at filling stations and outside many supermarkets (priced in litres).

Parking: This is a big problem in central London. Meters are slightly less expensive than NCP (multistorey) car parks, but some only allow parking for a maximum of two hours. Do not leave your car on a meter a moment longer than your time allows and do not return and insert more money once your time has run out – both are finable offences. Most meter parking is free after 6.30pm daily and all day Sunday, but always check on the meter.

Speed limits: Unless otherwise indicated these are: 30mph (50kph) in urban areas, 60mph (100kph) on normal roads away from built-up areas, 70mph (112kph) on motorways and dual carriageways.

Breakdown: The following organisations operate 24-hour breakdown assistance for members: AA, tel: 0800-887 766, www.theaa.com; RAC, tel: 0800-828 282, www.rac.co.uk.

E

Electricity

The standard current in Britain is 230-volt, 50-cycle AC. Plugs have three pins, so you need an adaptor.

Embassies

Australia: Australia House, Strand, WC2B; tel: 020-7379 4334; www.uk embassy.gov.au.

Canada: Macdonald House, 1 Grosvenor Square, W1; tel: 020-7258 6600; http://canada.embassyhome page.comeuropa.

Ireland: 17 Grosvenor Place, SW1X; tel: 020-7235 2171; www.embassyofire land.co.uk.

New Zealand: 80 Haymarket, SW1Y; tel: 020-7930 8422; www.nzembassy. com.

US: 24 Grosvenor Square, W1A; tel: 020-7499 9000; http://london.us embassy.gov.

Emergencies

For police, fire brigade or ambulance, dial **999** free from any telephone. To contact the police about a non-emergency, dial **101**.

Entry requirements

You need a valid passport (or any form of official identification if you are an EU citizen). Visas are not needed if you are from the US, a Commonwealth citizen or an EU national (or from most other European or South American countries). Health certificates are not required unless you have arrived from Asia, Africa or South America. If you wish to stay for a protracted period or apply to work, contact the UK Border Agency (www.ind.homeoffice.gov.uk).

G

Gay and lesbian

With Europe's largest gay and lesbian population, London has an abundance of bars, restaurants and clubs to cater for most tastes, with the scene focusing around Soho and Vauxhall. Clapham is another very gay-friendly area. For listings, consult the free gay weekly magazines *Boyz*, the *Pink Paper* and *QX*. Monthly magazines for sale include *Gay Times*, *Diva* and *Attitude*.

Useful contacts for advice and counselling include London Lesbian and Gay Switchboard (tel: 0300-330 0630; www.llgs.org.uk) and London Friend (tel: 020-7837 1674/3337; www.london-friend.org.uk).

H

Health and medical care

EU citizens can receive free treatment on producing a European Health Insurance Card. Citizens of other countries must pay, except for emergency treatment (always free). Major hospitals include Charing Cross Hospital (Fulham Palace Road, W6, tel: 020-8846 1234) and St Thomas's (Westminster Bridge Road, SE1, tel: 020-7188 7188). Guy's Hospital Dental Department is at Great Maze Pond, SE1, tel: 020-7188 8006. For the nearest hospital or doctor, ring nhs Direct, tel: 111. If you need medication outside normal business hours, visit

Bureau de change

Zafash 24-hour Pharmacy (233–5 Old Brompton Road; tel: 020-7373 2798).

I

Internet

Free Wi-fi internet access is becoming increasingly common, in coffee bars, hotels, pubs and bookstores. There are also many internet cafés, where you pay for use by the hour.

L

Left luggage

Most of the main railway stations have left-luggage departments where you can leave suitcases on a short-term basis, although all are extremely sensitive to potential terrorist bombs.

Lost property

For possessions lost on public transport or in taxis, contact Transport for London's central Lost Property office (tel: 0343-222 1234), or fill in an enquiry form, available from any London Underground station.

M

Media

Newspapers: Daily national papers include the *Daily Telegraph* and *The Times* (both right of centre politically), *The Independent* (in the middle) and *The Guardian* (left of centre). Most have Sunday equivalents. The *Finan-cial Times* is more business and finance oriented. Except for the *Daily Mirror*, the tabloids (*The Sun, Star, Mail* and *Express*) are right-wing. The free *Evening Standard* (Mon–Fri) is good for cinema and theatre listings.

Listings magazines: The free, weekly *Time Out* is the most comprehensive.

Television: The BBC is financed by annual TV licences; ITV, Channel 4 and Five are funded by advertising. There are also scores of digital, cable and satellite channels to choose from.

Radio: BBC stations include Radio 1 (98.8FM, pop), Radio 2 (89.2FM, easy listening), Radio 3 (91.3FM, classical music), Radio 4 (93.5FM, current affairs, plays, discussions, etc), BBC London (94.9FM, music, chat) and BBC World Service (648 kHz, news). Commercial stations include Capital FM (96.8FM, pop), Jazz FM (102.2FM) and Classic FM (100.9FM).

Money

Currency: The monetary unit is the pound sterling (£), divided into 100 pence (p). Bank notes: £5, £10, £20, £50. Coins: 1p, 2p, 5p, 10p, 20p, 50p, £1, £2. Some of London's large stores also accept euros.

Banks: Opening hours are 9.30am–4.30pm Monday to Friday, with Saturday morning banking common in shopping areas. Major British banks tend to offer similar exchange rates, so it is only worth looking around if you have large amounts of money to

Docklands Light Railway at Canary Wharf

change. Banks charge no commission on sterling traveller's cheques, and if a London bank is affiliated to your own bank, it will not charge for cheques in other currencies either. However, there will be a charge for changing cash into another currency. You will need ID such as a passport in order to change traveller's cheques.

ATMs: The easiest way to take out money is using an ATM (cashpoint or cash machine) using your bank card. The best rates are usually available this way. Cash machines can be found inside and outside banks, in supermarkets and some tube stations. ATMs are accessed using a numeric PIN code.

Credit cards: International credit cards are almost universally accepted in shops, restaurants and hotels. Signs at the entrance or next to the till should confirm which cards are accepted.

Currency exchange: Some high-street travel agents, such as Thomas Cook, operate bureaux de change at comparable rates. There are also private bureaux de change (some are open 24 hours), where rates are sometimes very low and commissions very high.

Tipping: In Britain it is customary to add 10 percent to the bill for service. Be careful, though, that you do not pay for service twice, since many restaurants add this (or more often 12.5 percent) to the bill automatically. Of course, if you are less than satisfied with the service, do not hesitate to leave a smaller tip, or none at all. You might also check with the waiting staff whether they get to keep the tips or whether the management pockets them instead.

O

Opening hours

Most shops open from 9 or 10am until 6 or 6.30pm. West End shops usually open late, until around 8pm, and later still on Thursday. Most shops open on Sundays, although with shorter hours.

P

Postal services

Most post offices open Mon–Fri 9am–5pm, Sat 9am–noon. Stamps are also available from some shops, usually newsagents, and from machines outside some post offices. There is a two-tier service: first class is supposed to reach a UK destination the next day, second class will take at least a day or two longer. London's main post office (24–8 William IV Street) is by Trafalgar Square, behind the church of St Martin-in-the-Fields and is open Mon–Fri 8am–6.30pm, Sat 9am–5.30pm.

The cost of sending a letter or parcel depends on weight and size.

Public holidays

1 January: New Year's Day
March/April: Good Friday; Easter Monday.
May: May Day (first Monday); Spring Bank Holiday (last Monday).

St Pancras station   *Trafalgar Square*

August: Summer Bank Holiday (last Monday).

25 December: Christmas Day.

26 December: Boxing Day.

Public transport

Underground (tube)

The fastest and easiest way to get around is by tube. Services run from 5.30am to just after midnight. Always retain your ticket after you have passed through the barrier; you will need it to exit. There is a flat rate of £4.50 for a single tube journey in any single zone. Oyster cards (see below) are a wise buy if you plan to travel a lot by tube (tel: 0343-222 1234; www.tfl.gov.uk).

Docklands Light Railway

The DLR runs from Bank and Tower Gateway to east and southeast London destinations. Tickets are the same type and cost as for the tube.

Rail

London's commuter rail network provides links to areas not on underground lines; travelcards are valid on rail services for journeys within the correct zones. Thameslink services run through the city centre, while the London Overground connects Richmond with Stratford via the north of the capital. Other services run out of London's major rail stations, including Waterloo, King's Cross, London Bridge, Victoria and Liverpool Street. For times and fares tel: 08457-48 49 50; www.nationalrail.co.uk.

Bus

If you are not in a hurry, travelling by bus is a good way of seeing London; the bus network is very comprehensive. The flat fare is £2.40. Again, an Oyster card is the best bet, as each journey then costs £1.40, and the total is price-capped at £4.40 per day. You can get a seven-day pass for £19.60. Night buses run all night on the most popular routes. Bus route maps are available at Travel Information Centres.

The iconic 'Routemaster' double-decker bus was introduced in London in 1956 and remained in general service until 2005. However, owing to Government legislation requiring full accessibility to public transport for wheelchair users by 2017, only two 'Heritage' routes, the no. 9 and no. 15, still use Routemasters.

Boat

Thames cruises are a great way to see the sights. Various routes run between Hampton Court and Barrier Gardens. There is a hop-on-hop-off River Rover pass (£17; www.citycruises.com).

Tickets and fares

Single tickets on London's transport networks are very expensive, so it's best to buy one of several multi-journey passes. London is divided into six fare zones, with zones 1–2 covering all of central London, and are priced according to which zone you travel in. Travelcards give unlimited travel on the

Black cab

tube, buses and DLR. A one-day travelcard for zones 1 and 2, off-peak (valid after 9.30am) costs £7.30. You can also buy three-day or seven-day cards. Oyster cards are smart cards that you charge up with credit (using cash or a credit card), then touch in on card readers at tube stations and on buses, so that an amount is deducted each time you use it. They are cheaper than travelcards if you only expect to travel a few times each day. Cards and Oysters can be bought from tube and DLR stations and from newsagents. Visitors can order them in advance from www.visit britaindirect.com. For full details of all fares, see www.tfl.gov.uk.

S

Smoking

Since July 2007 smoking in all enclosed public spaces, including pubs, clubs and bars (though not in outside beer gardens) has been banned.

Student travellers

International students can obtain various discounts at attractions, on travel services (including Eurostar) and in some shops, by showing a valid isic card; see www.isiccard.com for details.

T

Tax

Value-Added Tax (VAT), currently 20 percent, is levied on most goods for sale in Britain. Non-EU visitors may claim this back, when spending over a certain amount. A VAT-refund form, available from retailers, needs to be completed and shown to customs on departure, along with all relevant goods and receipts. Ask in shops or at the airport for full details or visit www. hmrc.gov.uk.

Taxis

Black cabs are licensed and display the charges on the meter. They can be hailed in the street if their 'for hire' sign is lit. There are also ranks at major train stations and at various points across the city, or you can order a cab on 0871-871 8710. All black cabs are wheelchair accessible. Some black cabs may be reluctant to go far south of the river.

Minicabs should only be hired by phone; they are not allowed to pick up passengers on the street. Reputable firms include: Addison Lee, tel: 0844-800 6677; www.addisonlee.com.

Telephones

London's UK dialling code is 020. To call from abroad, dial '44', the international access code for Britain, then 20 (the London code, with the initial '0' dropped), then the eight-digit individual number.

To phone abroad, dial 00 followed by the international code for the country you want, then the number: Australia (61); Ireland (353); US and Canada (1), etc.

Clock at the Royal Observatory *Duck Tours*

Despite the ubiquity of mobiles (cellphones), London still has a fair number of public phone boxes; most accept phonecards, which are widely available from post offices and newsagents in amounts from £1 to £20. At coin-operated phone boxes, the smallest coin accepted is 20p.

Useful numbers

Emergency – police, fire, ambulance: tel: 999
Operator (for difficulties in getting through): tel: 100
International Operator: tel: 155
Directory Enquiries (UK): tel: 118 500 or 118 888 or 118 811
International Directory Enquiries: tel: 118 505 or 118 866 or 118 899

Time

In winter, Great Britain is on Greenwich Mean Time, 8 hours ahead of Los Angeles, 5 hours ahead of New York and Montreal, and 10 hours behind Sydney. From the last Sunday in March to the last Sunday in October, clocks are put forward one hour.

Tour operators

The **Original Tour** (tel: 020-8877 1722; www.theoriginaltour.com) runs hop-on-hop-off bus routes in Central London with more than 90 different stops with commentaries available in a variety of languages. There is also a Kids' Club for 5- to 12-year-olds. Purchase tickets on the bus or in advance.

Duck Tours (tel: 020-7928 3132; www.londonducktours.co.uk) employ World War II amphibious vehicles, which leave from County Hall, then drive past famous London landmarks before taking to the water on the Thames. Good fun for children.

Tourist offices

The most useful tourist information office is the City of London Information Centre, St Paul's Churchyard, tel: 020-7332 1456, Mon–Sat 9.30am–5.30am, Sun 10am–4pm. There is another office in Greenwich and travel and tourist information is available at Holborn, Liverpool Street, Piccadilly, Kings Cross and Victoria stations. The London Information Line is another useful resource (tel: 08701-566 366; www.visitlondon.com).

W

Websites

In addition to the many websites listed in this book, the following are useful:
www.bbc.co.uk/london (BBC London)
www.thisislondon.com (*Evening Standard* site; useful listings)
www.streetmap.co.uk (address locator)
www.culture24.org.uk (up-to-date information on museum shows)

Weights and Measures

Although distances are still measured in miles, and drinks are served as pints, all goods must officially be sold in metric measurements.

BOOKS AND FILM

London has a literary tradition that permeates its streets. All over the city are blue plaques memorialising famous writers and there's barely a place that doesn't conjure up thoughts of all the Londons that have been written about; the back streets of Holborn recall Charles Dickens's novels while the genteel terraces of Bloomsbury evoke the spirit of Virginia Woolf. Pay tribute to great writers with a visit to Poet's Corner in Westminster Abbey, take inspiration from Hampstead Heath like John Keats and C.S. Lewis or just have a drink at one of Fitzrovia or Soho's many pubs that are steeped in literary history.

There's a big film scene too. Stargazers head to Leicester Square, where crowds line behind barriers to watch stars parade along red carpets to film premieres, but London's cinematic scene involves so much more. Film festivals are held regularly, celebrating incredibly diverse cinema from around the world and energetically striving to reach new audiences. The characterful independent, repertory and arthouse cinemas also show a broad range of films, so you will never be short of something to watch.

The home-grown film industry thrives too, with in-vogue London continuing to be a backdrop to multiple projects.

Books

Good companions
London: A Literary Companion by Peter Vansittart. A journey around the capital with the literary luminaries.
Secret London by Andrew Duncan. Uncovers London's hidden landscape from abandoned tube stations to the gentlemen's club.
The London Blue Plaque Guide by Nick Rennison. Details the lives of more than 700 individuals who have been commemorated with a blue plaque on their houses.
A Literary Guide to London by Ed Glinet. A very detailed, street-by-street guide to literary lives.
London on Film by Colin Sorensen. How the cinema has portrayed the city.

History
The Concise Pepys by Samuel Pepys. Read a first-hand account of the Great Fire of London and find out about daily life in 17th-century England.
Dr Johnson's London by Liza Picard. Brings 18th-century London to life.
London: The Biography by Peter Ackroyd. Anecdotal and entertaining history.
London: A Social History by Roy Porter. Less quirky than Ackroyd but a telling account of how badly the capital has been governed over the centuries.

28 Days Later

The Story of the British Museum by Marjorie Caygill. A fascinating tale, authoritatively told, featuring an astonishing variety of heroes and villains.
London Villages by John Wittich. A walker's notes on his travels through village London.
Thames: Sacred River by Peter Ackroyd. Social history of London's famous river.

Memoirs
The Shorter Pepys by Samuel Pepys. A distillation of 11 volumes of diaries describing London life, including the Great Fire and the plague, from 1660 to 1669.
84 Charing Cross Road by Helene Hanff. Touching book-lover's correspondence with a London book seller.
London Orbital by Iain Sinclair. A walk round the M25, exploring little-known parts of London's periphery.
The Oxford Book of London edited by Paul Bailey. A bran-dip of observations by famous visitors to London over eight centuries.

Art and Architecture
A Guide to London's Contemporary Architecture by Ken Allinson and Victoria Thornton. Covers buildings since the 1980s; black-and-white pictures.
London Under London by Richard Trench and Ellis Hillman. Traces the astonishing maze of railway lines, sewers and utilities that lies beneath the streets.

Film

London has long been a favoured setting for film-making. Some of the most successful spy thrillers, literary adaptations, musicals and romantic comedies ever made have been set and filmed in London. Years ago, Hollywood's vision of the city involved it being wreathed in fog, peopled by people who either spoke in clipped tones or dubious mock-Cockney; today, although there is a still a romanticised version of London popularised by Richard Curtis films such as *Notting Hill* and *Bridget Jones's Diary*, other films have gathered acclaim for their depictions of a grittier take on the city.

In the post-World War Two years, Ealing comedies such as *Passport to Pimlico* and *The Ladykillers* used atmospheric London settings to great effect, as did Hitchcock before them. The innovative 'swinging London' film makers of the 1960s (*Blowup, Alfie, Darling*) and more recently, auteurs like Mike Leigh (*Secrets and Lies*) and Gary Oldman (*Nil by Mouth*) have provided an edgier but equally evocative contribution to this tradition.

More recent popular home-grown fare, such as *28 Days Later*, *Bend it like Beckham*, *Shaun of the Dead* and *Kidulthood*, continue to prove the commercial strength of the London film-making scene. And of course, the evocative backdrops of the city continue to be used for period dramas such as *Elizabeth* and *Sweeney Todd*.

ABOUT THIS BOOK

This *Explore Guide* has been produced by the editors of Insight Guides, whose books have set the standard for visual travel guides since 1970. With top-quality photography and authoritative recommendations, these guidebooks bring you the very best routes and itineraries in the world's most exciting destinations.

BEST ROUTES

The routes in the book provide something to suit all budgets, tastes and trip lengths. As well as covering the destination's many classic attractions, the itineraries track lesser-known sights, and there are also excursions for those who want to extend their visit beyond the city centre. The routes embrace a range of interests, so whether you are an art fan, a gourmet, a history buff or have kids to entertain, you will find an option to suit.

We recommend reading the whole of a route before setting out. This should help you to familiarise yourself with it and enable you to plan where to stop for refreshments – options are shown in the 'Food and Drink' box at the end of each tour.

For our pick of the tours by theme, consult Recommended Routes for… (see pages 4–5).

INTRODUCTION

The routes are set in context by this introductory section, giving an overview of the destination to set the scene, plus background information on food and drink, shopping and more, while a succinct history timeline highlights the key events over the centuries.

DIRECTORY

Also supporting the routes is a Directory chapter, with a clearly organised A–Z of practical information, our pick of where to stay while you are there and select restaurant listings; these eateries complement the more low-key cafés and restaurants that feature within the routes and are intended to offer a wider choice for evening dining. Also included here are some nightlife listings and our recommendations for books and films about the destination.

ABOUT THE AUTHORS

Michael Macaroon is a writer who specialises in travel and the arts. He has lived in London for many years and, with the exception of its public transport system, enjoys all the city has to offer. He never tires of its old-fashioned boozers or its Indian takeaways, nor for that matter its over-elaborate Victorian theatres or white minimalist art galleries. Macaroon has contributed to several other guides for Insight, including *Explore Paris* and *Smart Guide Budapest*.

CONTACTING EDITORS

We would appreciate it if readers would alert us to errors or outdated information by writing to us at insight@apaguide.co.uk or APA Publications, PO Box 7910, London SE1 1WE, UK.

CREDITS

Explore London
Contributors: Michael Macaroon, Jackie Staddon and Hilary Weston
Commissioning Editor: Tom Stainer
Series Editor: Sarah Clark
Art Editor: Tom Smyth
Map Production: © OpenStreetMap contributors. Converted by Phoenix Mapping Ltd, updated by Apa Cartography Department
Production: Tynan Dean and Rebeka Davies
Photo credits: Alamy 136, 137; Capital Hotel 108/109; Corbis 20, 122; Corrie Wingate/Apa 88; Dreamstime 92; Fotolia 118/119; Getty Images 6/7T, 21, 124/125; Glyn Genin/Apa 78; Hyatt Hotels 110; iStock 93; La Caprice 112; Leonardo 102, 102/103, 103L, 104, 106, 106/107, 107L, 108, 109L; London Bridge Hotel 111; Lydia Evans/Apa 2ML, 2MC, 2MR, 2MR, 2MC, 2/3T, 4TL, 4MC, 4ML, 4BC, 5MR, 5MR, 6ML, 6MC, 6ML, 6MC, 6MR, 6MR, 8, 8/9T, 9B, 10, 10/11T, 11T, 11B, 12B, 12T, 13, 14, 14/15, 15L, 16/17, 17L, 18, 19L, 24/25(all), 26, 28, 28/29, 29L, 30, 31, 36, 40, 40/41, 42, 43L, 42/43, 44, 44/45, 45L, 46, 46/47, 47L, 48, 48/49, 49L, 50, 52, 52/53, 53L, 54L, 54/55, 55, 56, 57, 58/59, 59L, 60, 60/61, 61L, 62, 62/63, 63L, 64, 64/65, 65L, 66, 66/67, 67L, 69L, 72/73, 74, 74/75, 75L, 76, 78/79, 79L, 81, 82, 82/83, 83L, 84, 85, 86, 86/87, 87L, 88/89, 89L, 90, 94L, 94/95, 95, 96, 97, 98, 99L, 100MC, 100MR, 100MC, 100ML, 100/101T, 112/113, 113L, 115, 118, 119L, 126, 127, 128, 128/129, 129L, 130, 131, 132, 132/133, 133L, 134L, 134/135, 135; Ming Tang-Evans/Apa 1, 2ML, 5T, 5M, 9T, 16, 18/19, 27L, 26/27, 32, 34/35, 35L, 36/37, 39, 51, 58, 68, 68/69, 70, 71, 76/77, 77L, 80, 91, 98/99, 100ML, 116, 116/117, 117L, 120/121, 123; Public Domain 33, 34; Starwood Hotles & Resorts 100MR, 105; The Art Archive 22/23; The Goring Hotel 114; Tom Smyth 37L, 38, 41L
Cover credits: Main: Trafalgar Square, *Corbis*; BL: Beefeaters *Corbis*; Back Cover: (Left) Greenwich Park *Lydia Evans/Apa* (Right): Bus *Dreamstime*

Printed by CTPS – China
© 2014 Apa Publications (UK) Ltd
All Rights Reserved
First Edition 2014

DISTRIBUTION

Worldwide
APA Publications GmbH & Co. Verlag KG (Singapore branch)
7030 Ang Mo Kio Ave 5, 08-65 Northstar @ AMK, Singapore 569880
Email: apasin@singnet.com.sg

UK and Ireland
Dorling Kindersley Ltd (a Penguin Company)
80 Strand, London, WC2R 0RL, UK
Email: customerservice@uk.dk.com

US
Ingram Publisher Services
One Ingram Blvd, PO Box 3006, La Vergne, TN 37086-1986
Email: ips@ingramcontent.com

Australia
Universal Publishers
PO Box 307, St. Leonards NSW 1590
Email: sales@universalpublishers.com.au

New Zealand
Brown Knows Publications
11 Artesia Close, Shamrock Park, Auckland, New Zealand 2016
Email: sales@brownknows.co.nz

INDEX

MAP LEGEND

- ● Start of tour
- ➔ Tour & route direction
- ❶ Recommended sight
- ❷ Recommended restaurant/café

- ★ Place of interest
- ❶ Tourist information
- ⊖⊖ Underground/DLR station
- 🚊 Mainline railway station
- 🚶 Statue/monument
- ✉ Main post office
- 🚌 Main bus station
- – – – Ferry route

- Park
- Important building
- Hotel
- Transport hub
- Shopping / market
- Pedestrian area
- Urban area